W9-CJK-361

The World of
Giotto

TIME
LIFE
BOOKS
®

TIME-LIFE LIBRARY OF ART

The World of Giotto

c. 1267 - 1337

by Sarel Eimerl
and
the Editors of TIME-LIFE BOOKS

TIME-LIFE BOOKS, New York

TIME-LIFE BOOKS

FOUNDER: Henry R. Luce 1898-1967

Editor-in-Chief: Hedley Donovan
Chairman of the Board: Andrew Heiskell
President: James R. Shepley
Group Vice President: Rhett Austell

Vice Chairman: Roy E. Larsen

MANAGING EDITOR: Jerry Korn
Assistant Managing Editors: Ezra Bowen, David Maness,
Martin Mann, A. B. C. Whipple
Planning Director: Oliver E. Allen
Art Director: Sheldon Cotler
Chief of Research: Beatrice T. Dobie
Director of Photography: Melvin L. Scott
Senior Text Editor: Diana Hirsh
Assistant Art Director: Arnold C. Holeywell

PUBLISHER: Joan D. Manley
General Manager: John D. McSweeney
Business Manager: John Steven Maxwell
Sales Director: Carl G. Jaeger
Promotion Director: Paul R. Stewart
Public Relations Director: Nicholas Benton

TIME-LIFE LIBRARY OF ART
SERIES EDITOR: Robert Morton
Editorial Staff for *The World of Giotto:*
Associate Editor: Diana Hirsh
Picture Editor: Jane Scholl
Designer: Paul Jensen
Assistant Designer: Leonard Wolfe
Staff Writers: Tim Carr, Frank Kendig, John Stanton
Chief Researcher: Martha T. Goolrick
Researchers: Jane Alexander, Judith Levenson,
Patricia Maye, Jenifer Ratliff

EDITORIAL PRODUCTION
Production Editor: Douglas B. Graham
Assistant Production Editor: Gennaro C. Esposito
Quality Director: Robert L. Young
Assistant Quality Director: James J. Cox
Copy Staff: Rosalind Stubenberg (chief), Muriel Kotselas,
Florence Keith
Picture Department: Dolores A. Littles, Barbara Simon
Art Assistant: Nanci Earle

About the Author

Sarel Eimerl, a graduate of Oxford living in the U.S., is a novelist who has written books on scientific subjects as well as the history of art. He was co-author of *The Primates* in the LIFE Nature Library, and of *The Physician* in the LIFE Science Library.

The Consulting Editor

H. W. Janson is Professor of Fine Arts at New York University, where he is also Chairman of the Department of Fine Arts at Washington Square College. Among his numerous publications are his *History of Art* and *The Sculpture of Donatello.*

The Consultant for This Book

James H. Stubblebine is Professor of Art History at Rutgers University. The author of numerous articles on early Italian paintings, he has also published books on Guido da Siena and Giotto's Arena Chapel frescoes.

On the Slipcase

Giotto's mastery of form and human emotion is brilliantly evident in this detail from an Arena Chapel fresco, which shows the kneeling Mary Magdalen reaching lovingly toward the Risen Christ *(scene 37, page 125).*

End Papers

Figures from the Arena Chapel in Padua depict man's virtues and vices.
Front: The seven *Virtues: (left to right)—Hope, Charity, Justice, Faith, Fortitude, Prudence* and *Temperance.*
Back: The *Vices (left to right)—Wrath, Injustice, Envy, Idolatry, Despair, Folly* and *Inconstancy.*

The following individuals and departments of Time Inc. helped to produce this book: photographer Dmitri Kessel; Editorial Production, Norman Airey; Library, Benjamin Lightman; Picture Collection, Doris O'Neil; Photographic Laboratory, George Karas; TIME-LIFE News Service, Murray J. Gart; Correspondents Ann Natanson and Erik Amfitheatrof (Rome), Victor Velen (Florence), Maria Vincenza Aloisi (Paris), Barbara Moir (London), Friso Endt (Amsterdam).

© 1967 Time Inc. All rights reserved.
Published simultaneously in Canada. Reprinted 1974.
Library of Congress catalogue card number 67-23024.
School and library distribution by Silver Burdett Company, Morristown, New Jersey.

Contents

6

I

The Conquest of Form

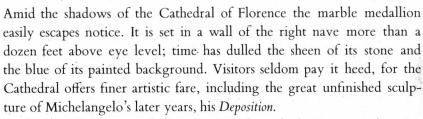

Amid the shadows of the Cathedral of Florence the marble medallion easily escapes notice. It is set in a wall of the right nave more than a dozen feet above eye level; time has dulled the sheen of its stone and the blue of its painted background. Visitors seldom pay it heed, for the Cathedral offers finer artistic fare, including the great unfinished sculpture of Michelangelo's later years, his *Deposition*.

The medallion, nevertheless, merits a long look. In its unobtrusive way it is a monument of Western art. The man it commemorates is shown as he surely would have liked to be recalled: in the act of creating one of his works. The face beneath the close-cropped curls is rugged. The body is thickset. Of pretension there is little, of strength and assurance much. Clearly this is a man in command of his resources.

How true the likeness is to his real self is uncertain. But the sentiments inscribed in Latin in the plaque below are unequivocal:

> *I am he through whose merit the lost art of painting was revived; whose hand was as faultless as it was compliant. What my art lacked nature herself lacked; to none other was it given to paint more or better. . . . But what need is there for words? I am Giotto, and my name alone tells more than a lengthy ode.*

Few artists anywhere, of any era, have evoked so awesome a tribute, and not the least remarkable part of it is the fact that it was written some 150 years after Giotto died, at a time when works more advanced than his in technique, more polished in execution, more spectacular in appearance, were pouring forth to herald the High Renaissance. The prime mover of that splendid age, Lorenzo de' Medici himself, ordered this testimonial to Giotto; it was at his behest that Benedetto da Maiano, the sculptor who some believe guided the young Michelangelo's first ventures in marble, fashioned the medallion in 1490. And it was Lorenzo, a poet himself, who asked Angelo Poliziano, one of the best poets of the Renaissance, to compose the inscription.

Conceivably such retrospective homage to Giotto could have been a mere token. Graceful gestures came effortlessly to men of the Renaissance;

More than a century after Giotto died, the Renaissance paid tribute to the man regarded as the grandfather of Italian art in this commemorative medallion in the Cathedral of Florence, where Giotto was buried. Although Giotto's chief forte was painting, he is shown here fitting a tile chip into a small mosaic of a head of Christ.

Benedetto da Maiano: *Portrait of Giotto*, 1490

7

they would have felt it fitting in any event to do honor to a founding father of the art that enriched their lives. But their veneration of Giotto was, in fact, genuine; moreover, it was no greater than the esteem accorded him in his own time—and throughout the 600 years since.

From his day to ours, to speak of Giotto has been to speak in superlatives. In the midstream of his productivity in the early 14th Century, his illustrious friend Dante acclaimed him by name in the *Divine Comedy,* pronouncing him supreme in his field. In the 15th Century, Lorenzo Ghiberti, creator of the *Gates of Paradise* of the Baptistery of Florence, declared that "Giotto saw in art that which others failed to perceive," and from his towering eminence Leonardo da Vinci observed: "After him art declined."

Later eras—and revolutions in art—have brought no diminution of Giotto's stature. "When I see Giotto's frescoes at Padua," wrote Henri Matisse in 1908, "I do not trouble to find out which scene of the life of Christ is before me, for I understand at once the feeling which radiates from it, and which is instinct in the line, the composition, the color. The title would only confirm my impression." Giotto's power to enchant has survived even the most savage onslaughts on the representational art he pioneered. Painters dedicated to demolishing the human figure, to dissolving the substance of form, recognize by these very efforts the extent of Giotto's genius as a builder of form. "The terrible plebeian beauty of this Tuscan wonder worker," as the modern Italian master Carlo Carrà has called it, continues to cast its spell.

The measure of an artist's effectiveness is his ability to make contact with the viewer. This holds true whether he deals in traditional subject matter or no subject matter; whether he wields a brush according to preconceived plan or drips paint onto a canvas willy-nilly; whether the medium he uses is tempera, oil, watercolor or bits of paper and wood. "The one and only quality denied a work of art throughout the ages is privacy," the museum director Francis Henry Taylor once wrote. "Unless participation is allowed the spectator, it becomes a hopeless riddle and ceases to be a work of art at all."

Giotto's greatness lay in his recognition that a painting could be a shared experience, and in his repeated achievement of that end. After six centuries of painters who have performed the same feat, often brilliantly, such an accomplishment may seem less than momentous. But it was Giotto who led the way. In his hands, paintings for the first time projected people and emotions and situations with which the onlooker could readily identify.

For the most part, painting prior to Giotto had served two purposes: it was purely decorative or it was frankly dogmatic. Wealthy Romans who had the interiors of their villas adorned with imaginary vistas sought no more than the sheer sensuous delight of the eye. With the Christian era, painting became a means of propagating and strengthening the faith. From the minuscule illustrations on the pages of manuscripts produced in monasteries, as well as from the depictions of religious themes on the walls and altars of churches, the viewer could draw doctrinal guidance, a knowledge of Scripture and sacred legend and, perhaps most important, a proper sense of reverence. Sometimes, indeed, the painting itself functioned as an icon to be venerated.

Giotto made no attempt to break with the tradition that art must be a handmaiden of the Church. But he infused his art with a new humanity. Instead of using the glittering gold background which previous painters had employed to create an aura of supernatural mystery, he placed his figures in settings of hills, meadows and houses familiar to any Italian. Whereas previous painters had disposed their figures with little regard for their relationships, he arranged people in a meaningful, natural manner; moreover he grouped them along the lower half of the picture, so that the viewer could look at, rather than up to, the scene before him. The subtlety of these innovations was not lost on Giotto's contemporaries; he was proclaiming his belief that a man and his faith must meet on a comprehensible level.

In his portrayal of individuals Giotto also parted sharply with the past. Representations of the human face in earlier paintings had given it an expressionless stare; he invested it with grief, fear, pity, joy or other emotions to which the viewer could respond with instant understanding. Above all, Giotto endowed his people with flesh and blood. Earlier painters had provided the human form with monumental proportions, overpowering majesty, and often elegance and grace; essentially, however, the figures in these works bore as much semblance to reality as gigantic paper cutouts.

Giotto's people had the down-to-earth solidity of peasants. Their feet were unmistakably on the ground; they had weight and roundness and three-dimensional believability. The only painted figures that approached them in naturalism were those of Greek and Roman times; it was for this reason that Giotto was credited after his death, by Renaissance admirers newly infatuated with antiquity, with having revived "the lost art of painting." But advance, rather than restoration, was Giotto's purpose. To construct a credible human form was not enough; to be thoroughly lifelike, it had to occupy credible space.

By the skillful distribution of light and shadow, Giotto gave his figures a depth which cut into the space around them; the figures themselves served as space markers. He then further defined the space by the clarity and logic with which he arranged his figures in relation to one another and to their setting. Earlier painters had tended either to stack their figures like so many pieces of cordwood or to leave them simply floating—suspended, as it were, in some vast, boundless chemical solution. Giotto not only anchored his figures to earth but suggested measurable distances between them. Although the laws of perspective were not worked out with mathematical exactness until the 15th Century, decades before then he showed his intuitive grasp of the rational disposition of forms in space.

Such technical prowess alone would have ensured Giotto's enduring fame. But he was also a master storyteller and a superb stage manager. And above all he had a genius for simplicity. He never yielded to the temptation to overdo. The hallmark of his work is economy and understatement; his truths required no embellishment.

His effect on his own day and age was electric. Whatever their degree of sophistication, spectators felt that they could reach out and touch

ARENA CHAPEL, PADUA

According to the writer Boccaccio, Giotto, though a genius, was as ugly a man as Italy was ever likely to produce. Although no known contemporary portrait of Giotto exists, scholars believe that the figure above—a detail from the *Last Judgment* in the Arena Chapel *(page 129)* —is a self-portrait. His face and white cap outlined in the dark contours typical of his style, Giotto has portrayed himself as a sturdy and not unhandsome fellow.

Giotto's people, walk among them, commune with them. The theme of the work might be Scriptural, but it had an undeniable application to everyday life. Returning from a scrutiny of Giotto's frescoes in Florence in 1874, the great English critic John Ruskin exclaimed: "He painted the Madonna and St. Joseph and the Christ—yes, by all means, if you choose to call them so—but essentially, Mamma, Papa, and the Baby." Giotto had, singlehanded, effected a fundamental breakthrough in art: he had elevated painting from the service of symbolism and made it a mirror of mankind.

Today the admirers of Giotto are many, but they are far from preponderant. To a modern eye his art may appear crude by contrast to that of later titans. Next to the musculature of a figure by Michelangelo or the anatomical perfection of a figure by Leonardo, a figure by Giotto seems cloddish and shapeless; alongside the swirling movement of a scene by Rubens, a scene by Giotto seems static; the richness of Titian's palette makes Giotto's colors look flat. Nevertheless, such comparisons are pointless: Giotto prepared the soil that nourished all the rest.

There are those who, while aware of Giotto's primary role in art, view him through a blur of bias. The secular spirit of the 20th Century finds a certain tedium in traditional religious art. The footsore tourist, having trudged through 20 Italian churches and gazed at 20 depictions of the Annunciation, the Nativity or the Adoration, may be overcome by a sense of sameness, whether the painter be an acknowledged master or some perfunctory craftsman with a talent only for imitation.

But beneath the apparent repetitiveness there is, in fact, astonishing variety. The conventions that governed the presentation of devotional themes did not deter the gifted artist from expressing himself in his own way. Like the subsequent painters of landscape, history, genre or portraits, he managed to shed a great deal of light not only on shifting artistic styles but on the temper of the time and place in which he lived.

One of the most familiar themes in Christian art, the Madonna and Child, provides a case in point. In the diversity of the treatment of this subject over the centuries can be clearly traced the changing theological climate of Christendom. The orthodoxy of the Eastern Church was so strict that the Byzantine artist, making his preparatory sketches, might have at his elbow some cleric versed in doctrinal fine points; and this rigidity was reflected in a Madonna shown aloft in a remote firmament, a wholly unapproachable being, incorporeal yet overwhelming, intended to strike awe in the beholder. Concurrently, a somewhat less forbidding but still austere Madonna appeared in the churches of Western Europe, crowned and enthroned—the Queen of Heaven and Mother of God.

During the Middle Ages, a special cult developed around the Virgin Mary: she came to be regarded as the principal intercessor for sinful mankind. In the painted representations a new softness suffused her features, a new tenderness marked her manner. Her figure was now recognizably feminine; she no longer held the Christ Child at stiff arm's length, but cradled or nursed Him; the Child was now recognizably an infant and not, as earlier painters had made him appear, a little old man. Later this Madonna was transformed into a Madonna of Humility, seated on the ground, and still later into a Madonna of Sorrows, sad-eyed, brooding, foreseeing the suffering her Son would endure.

Implicit in all these variations was a growing tendency to humanize religion. Within the broadening guidelines furnished by the theologians the painters could give fuller play to their own ideas. Giotto depicted the Madonna as an earthy farm woman; French court painters saw her as a svelte aristocrat, dressed and bejewelled in the current high fashion; the Germans preferred her as a plump blonde hausfrau. She was variously shown at ease before a hearth or tucked in a cozy bed, surrounded by the rocks and trees of the countryside or seated within the shelter of a rose garden. The symbolism was ever-present: white roses, for example, signified purity, and red roses martyrdom. At the same time the symbols gave the painter an opportunity to experiment with plant forms, domestic interiors and the minutiae of everyday life.

Long after art had become predominantly secular, the depiction of the Madonna continued to challenge the painter's imagination. With the spread of the Gospel beyond Europe, distinctive racial and national characteristics began to emerge in her portrayals. Mexican artists envisioned her as an Aztec maiden, the Chinese as an almond-eyed lady at a lantern festival; the Maori dressed her in long grass skirts and the Africans made her a Negro, sometimes with heavy coils of beads around her neck and with the Christ Child slung on her back. Modern painters have made her the repository of their hard-won personal styles or inner conflicts. On the white-tiled walls of the chapel at Vence, Matisse presented the Madonna as a stark outline in black—a giant mother-figure with ovoid head, faceless and featureless. One of Salvador Dali's studies for his *Madonna of Port Lligat* shows the Madonna with a cleft head, sitting suspended over a surrealist sea.

The unlimited choices open to today's artist—among them his freedom to decide whether to paint religious or secular themes or sheer abstractions—were not available to the artist of Giotto's time. Art was at the beck and call of the Church, and whatever individual expression its practitioner achieved was achieved within that framework.

Occasionally, under the stimulus of rising civic pride, the officials of an Italian city might commission a painter to help beautify a public building; as private fortunes increased, he might be hired to decorate the palazzo of a newly affluent family. By and large, however, his talents were channeled into Church projects. In such endeavors as the building of a cathedral, a local government might contribute resources of money and labor, and a local banker might donate an entire chapel. But it was the Church—through a bishop, a cardinal, or often the pope himself—that was the initiator and arbiter of artistic enterprise.

This central role of the Church in art can best be understood in the broader context of its central role in all of medieval life. The presence of the Church was as pervasive in temporal matters as in the spiritual realm. It asserted this power as an inherent right; it exercised the power by reason of its vast wealth, efficient bureaucracy and monolithic structure. Moreover, it existed in a relative vacuum, for strong governments responsive to laymen were still rare. On the Italian peninsula, turmoil was endemic; few temporal regimes, whether of emperor, king, provincial despot or elected republican leader, achieved any degree of longevity. The Church remained the great constant, encompassing all men whatever their political or social or economic differences. It stood as the one great force to be relied upon and to be reckoned with.

Medieval people felt the imprint of the Church on every aspect of their lives from birth until death. A child had to be baptized to be recognized as a member of society. The method and substance of his schooling were controlled by clerics; if he went on to a university, he had to become a member of one of the minor orders of the Church and accept the discipline of ecclesiastical courts. If he became a guild apprentice, he acquired a special patron saint and bound himself to perform periodic religious duties. If he grew prosperous enough to engage in commerce, he was guided by Church pronouncements on fair prices and interest rates. In general he conducted himself with the awareness that violation of Church rules could bring excommunication—a punishment that would deprive him not only of the sacraments but of his political and legal rights as well.

Yet any impression that people of the Middle Ages spent most of their time in prayer and pious acts would be misleading. Life was also lusty, licentious, brawling, violent; the material vied with the spiritual. There were many within the religious hierarchy itself who enjoyed the fleshpots—a fact which in turn bred considerable cynicism in the laity. They could see no exemplar of virtue or high ethics in the parish priest who ran an alehouse or the bishop who gloried in war and the hunt and lived sumptuously on the tithes exacted from the faithful. "It often happens," Pope Innocent III acknowledged in 1215, "that bishops, by reason of their manifold preoccupations, fleshly pleasures and bellicose leanings, and from other causes, not least the poverty of their spiritual training and lack of pastoral zeal, are unfitted to proclaim the word of God and govern the people."

Periodically, the Church attempted to clean house; and sometimes a single individual became the vessel of spiritual renewal. Such a man was Francis of Assisi, who appeared on the Italian scene during Innocent's reign. By the time of his death in 1226 he had set Christian thinking on a new course. He opened windows that had long been closed and admitted the air and sun; he banished the sense of gloom that had pervaded Christianity and supplanted it with joy. Up to then the faithful had been taught that their brief span on earth was but an insignificant prelude to eternity, and that in the inexorable advance toward this outcome they were but anonymous marchers. Francis did not believe that the prospect of the next world should cloud man's vision of this world; he saw an inherent harmony between the realm of the spirit and the realm of physical reality. The effects of Francis' teachings extended deep into the future, touching the lives and actions of many people in many lands. In Italy itself, a few generations later, his legacy helped make possible the revolution in art wrought by Giotto—and indeed much of the creative effort that shaped the Renaissance.

As a rule, accounts of the lives of saints have had only brief popular

VATICAN LIBRARY, ROME

Episodes from the lives of saints, described in illuminated manuscripts, provided the medieval reader with a wealth of information about his world. Books like the *Golden Legend* (from which the page above comes), taught history, geography and biography, as well as morality. Written by the Dominican Archbishop of Genoa, Jacopo da Voragine, and organized to be read in daily installments, it guided readers through every Christian epoch and continent in sprightly stories of canonized men and women from all walks of life.

appeal. They have been scrupulously recorded, dutifully perused, then relegated to church archives. An indication of the tenacity of St. Francis' grip on men's hearts lies in the frequency with which his life story —fact and legend intertwined—has been told and retold. Several of his companions set down their own accounts in loving detail soon after he died. These versions, which seem to have stressed Francis' simple idealism, his commitment to poverty and his abhorrence of formal organization, hardly suited the purposes of his successors, who were busily engaged in building a rich and complex institution. Thirty-seven years after his death a new, official life story appeared, and shortly thereafter the first biographies were deliberately destroyed. The author of the official version was Bonaventura, the powerful minister-general of the Franciscan order; from his book emerged a Francis more in keeping with what the order had become—an organization that, in truth, the founder would not have recognized. But the powerful memories of the sweetness of Francis' character would not die; after about 60 more years, yet another volume began to be circulated: *I Fioretti di San Francesco (The Little Flowers of St. Francis)*—a collection of his sermons and sayings and the anecdotes about him that the people most cherished.

I t was this gentle yet zealous man who was immortalized by the artists. Apart from Scripture itself, few sources of material have been more enthusiastically mined by painters, for the events of the saint's life and legend seemed to lend themselves especially to their art. Two incidents in particular caught the artists' attention. One was miraculous: the appearance on Francis' body of Christ's wounds, the stigmata, following a vision of the Crucifixion. The other was mundane, dealing with a sermon the gentle Francis was said to have preached to birds gathered around him as he stood in a meadow. The fascination that St. Francis held for medieval painters may itself have been a significant influence on art; some scholars see more than coincidence in the fact that only after his death did painting begin to take its place with sculpture and architecture as a major art. This is perhaps debatable; the painters' preoccupation with the saint is not. Evidences of it fill the churches and museums of all Europe. One of its earliest manifestations was the great fresco cycle about him in the basilica built in his name at his birthplace and resting place at Assisi—still today a magnet for a million visitors a year.

In its essentials, the story of St. Francis can be quickly told. The son of a prosperous cloth merchant, he lived the pleasure-bent life of a well-to-do young blade until, at about the age of 20, he was felled by a severe illness. It is not unusual for an enforced confinement to inspire a meditative mood; in Francis' case, however, it produced a complete revulsion against the easy comfort of his former ways and a decision to embrace a life of poverty as bare as that of the Apostles.

Francis did not forget his intention once he had regained his health. To learn true humility, he began to fraternize with the beggars whose pleas for alms he had once cursed and the lepers from whom he had turned in loathing. One day, at prayer in a chapel near Assisi, he thought he heard Christ speaking to him, accepting his life as a holy offering. When he returned to town, his face was so haggard and his

FOGG ART MUSEUM, HARVARD UNIVERSITY, BEQUEST OF HERVEY E. WETZEL

Although he was a personal friend and warm admirer of St. Francis, the Spanish monk who became St. Dominic (pictured above in a panel painting) established an order of preachers and educators that soon came to rival the Franciscans. The orders differed mainly in that the Dominicans stressed scholarship and intellectual activity while the Franciscans favored compassion and good works. Both built churches, monasteries, convents, schools and hospitals that generations of artists labored to beautify.

mind so bemused that boys gathered around him in the public square shouting, "A madman! A madman!" Francis' father shared the normal bourgeois regard for the proprieties, and when he heard of his son's unconventional behavior he threatened to disinherit the young man, and asked the local bishop to give him a talking-to.

Summoned before this dignitary, Francis—in a stirring scene that many a painter would subsequently dramatize—stripped off his clothes and declared, "Listen, everyone, and understand it well: Until now I have called Pietro Bernardone my father; but now that I intend to serve the Lord I am returning to this man all the money that has caused him such a pother, and all the clothes that were his property; and from now on I shall say 'Our Father which art in Heaven,' instead of 'my father, Pietro Bernardone.' "

The words "such a pother" vividly expressed the new Francis' profound contempt for material possessions and especially for money—"dung," he once called it. Henceforth he owned nothing; his one garment was a ragged gown girt with a rope. He lived anywhere, in hovels, in the woods, sustaining himself on the random charity of well-wishers. He began to rebuild some chapels near Assisi that had fallen into disrepair. In time, with a growing band of followers, he expanded his calling to tend the sick, help the poor and preach the Gospel in the towns and countryside of Central Italy, speaking in the homely images and everyday terms of the vernacular. The impact on common folk may be imagined; most were inured to neglect by their priests, and, as for the Holy Writ, they were accustomed to having it intoned at them in incomprehensible Latin.

By a curious turn of history, Francis and his friars were not alone in their itinerant mission. A Spanish monk named Dominic had felt a similar call, and his preaching friars were also out among the people. Dominic, too, was to be canonized, and his order, too, would grow into a vast and affluent network; by Giotto's time, the Dominicans and Franciscans would be arch-rivals, competing for power within the Church hierarchy and trying to outdo each other in the splendor of their churches and monasteries.

Between the founders themselves there were consequential differences. Dominic had undertaken his task specifically to stamp out heresy; he had had years of theological training at a university, and he employed reason to sway his hearers. Francis certainly did not condone heresy; he had received papal sanction—although a rather reluctant one —for his labors in 1210. Still, some who might otherwise have been labeled heretic found shelter within the ranks of the early Franciscans. Francis, furthermore, had scant use for formal education, fearing that it would create barriers between him and the people. He spoke to them not from the mind but from the heart.

Francis preached that the beauty of nature was God-given and therefore to be enjoyed; that all the things of the world—animate and inanimate—were God's creations, and therefore kin; that all men were brothers. And since they were brothers, they must deal with one another as equals, as individuals, each with his own private hopes and

BIBLIOTECA MEDICEA LAURENTIANA, FLORENCE

This illumination, which shows a Florentine merchant bargaining with two customers over his grain tubs *(top)* and recording a transaction in his books *(below),* is from a 14th Century ledger book listing grain prices in Italy. Such documents have enabled modern economists to reconstruct many of the facts of life in medieval Italian cities. It is known, for example, that grain, a vital staple, was sold by the *staio,* a 39-pound measure, each of which normally cost 12 silver florins. Florence's population exploded from 45,000 inhabitants in 1281 to 90,000 in 1338, causing constant anxiety over both the supply and cost of grain.

agonies. In the relations between human beings the binding force was love—love born of the knowledge that Christ resided within all of them. The Christ described by Francis was not the terrifying ruler of the cosmos whose Word could be conveyed only through a priesthood. Rather, as Francis constantly reminded his listeners: "Your God is of your flesh, He lives in your nearest neighbor, in every man."

This was the Christ whom Giotto, some decades later, would depict —a figure of familiar dimensions, as much of the earth as Giotto's farmwoman Madonna, a man to be loved, not feared. There was more that Giotto took from the preachings of St. Francis: his compassion for humanity and his simplicity. No less important, Giotto followed Francis' injunction to behold and savor the world around him.

Giotto's world was, first, the region of Tuscany. In a country replete with natural beauty, it is one of the most beautiful areas, a harmony of hills and valleys, green with cypress and pine. Second, Giotto's world was the city of Florence—not his birthplace, but for much of his lifetime his home. In the last years of the 13th Century, when his star was on the rise, Florence had already begun to display the character and qualities which, in the next two centuries, would make it economically and culturally pre-eminent, the financial capital of Europe and the core of the Renaissance.

The city's location on a main trade route between northern and southern Europe, the vigorous enterprise of its wool and grain merchants, the shrewd manipulations of its moneylenders—all these were bringing it immense riches and a bustling economy. Its new men of wealth, however, were also men of broad vision. By the time Giotto was a young man, the growing city boasted scores of commercial companies and banking houses. But it also had abacus schools to prepare boys for careers in trade, well-run hospitals, paved streets, and ordinances against unsanitary butchering and against the smoke nuisance from burning coal. In 1296 the construction of the Duomo, the huge Cathedral, was begun, and plans were afoot for other churches and public buildings that would enhance the city's splendor.

Politically, the Florentines were the freest of all Europeans. They had withstood the occupation forces of the Holy Roman Empire and incursions by papal armies, and were now flourishing under a form of republican government that, although dominated by the aristocratic and wealthy, gave some voice to artisans and shopkeepers. Even the poorest inhabitants were guaranteed some rights: an ordinance passed in 1293 imposed severe penalties on magnates or nobles who committed acts of violence against the common people.

The Florentines were cantankerous, contentious, ever ready—sometimes even anxious—for a fight, whether between local factions or against a common outside foe. With their characteristic mixture of hard sense and gentle sensibility, they had largely forgotten St. Francis' strictures against striving for material gain, but they passionately embraced his assessment of basic human worth, and moved ever more purposefully in pursuit of individualism. The city was on the brink of greatness, and Giotto stood ready to receive his share.

AMERICAN NUMISMATIC SOCIETY, NEW YORK

In the 13th Century, the privilege of coining was granted to cities only by the Emperor. In 1235, Florence, without obtaining imperial permission, boldly minted a new coin—the silver florin, worth 12 silver pennies of the traditionally authorized currency. It proved a far more convenient monetary unit for larger transactions, and in 1252 the city devised a still more valuable coin, the gold florin *(above)*, worth 240 pennies. Bearing a picture of St. John the Baptist, Florence's patron saint, on one side, and a lily, the city's emblem, on the other side, the gold florin soon became the standard currency of international trade.

The Early Masters

Late in the 12th Century, art in Italy began to emerge from the cloistered halls of monasteries and the rich seclusion of private chapels where only the privileged few could see it, and to blaze forth in public. Painting, once virtually limited to illuminated manuscript pages, developed in both size and narrative detail. To meet the needs of a rapidly expanding Church more and larger religious buildings were built, and artists used their growing skills to enliven the cold stone interiors with larger and more dramatic works. Most of these paintings were on wooden panels (sometimes on several panels joined together) that were set up as decorations on church altars. Although panel painting had existed in Byzantium for centuries, it was not widely adopted in Italy until the 12th and 13th Centuries. Most importantly, Italian artists began to endow their painting with a warmth, a reality and a feeling of direct communication with the spectator that was new.

These painters, about whose lives and careers almost nothing is known, were creating a functional art. They were commissioned at first to paint crucifixes. Later, they added Madonna-and-Child scenes, then episodes from the lives of saints to their repertoire. And although their art was restricted in subject matter and intended primarily to instruct the worshiper, these anonymous artists began to display the individuality that helped to set the scene for such giants as Giotto and the Renaissance masters.

The steadfastly staring eyes and flat, unrounded face of this Christ, from a 12th Century crucifix shown in its entirety on the next page, are typical stylizations of early Italian painters, who stressed His divine rather than human qualities.

Pisa Crucifix No. 15, detail, late 12th Century

Pisa Crucifix No. 15, late 12th Century

MUSEO NAZIONALE DI SAN MATTEO, PISA

The first type of panel painting to evolve in Italian art was the crucifix, often painted on a monumental scale. The two shown here, both of which are about 12 feet tall, adorned churches in Pisa. Pisan artists were fond of vivid narration and flanked their crucifixes with richly illustrated scenes. But despite their skill, their names are usually unrecorded and their panels are often identified only by museum catalogue numbers.

Pisa No. 15 (left), like most early crucifixes, depicted a Christ who appeared to be still alive, and superior to the agonies of the Cross. There is no mortal pain in this Christ; eyes opened and body erect, He triumphs over death. Scholars call this representation *Christus Triumphans*.

Pisa No. 20 (right) is the earliest known *Christus Patiens*, the Suffering Christ. He is portrayed as a human being in agony; pain knots His brow; His body slumps.

In this respect *Pisa No. 20* was a daring departure from tradition, and the same change in point of view, partly inspired by St. Francis' emphasis on Christ's suffering, is shown in the different treatment of the side scenes. In *Pisa No. 15,* for example, half of these scenes show events that took place before the Crucifixion; in *Pisa No. 20,* for the first time in Italian art, all the episodes follow the Crucifixion. Thus, both the portrayal of Christ and the pictorial narrative stress the fact of Christ's death and emphasize His sacrifice.

Pisa Crucifix No. 20, early 13th Century

MUSEO NAZIONALE DI SAN MATTEO, PISA

COLLECTION GEORGE R. HANN, SEWICKLEY, PENNSYLVANIA

Bigallo Master: *Madonna and Child Enthroned,* second quarter of the 13th Century

Coincident with a rise in popular interest in the Madonna, a second type of panel painting developed that was dedicated to her. The panel shown at left was painted by the Bigallo Master, so called because his work is known only from a crucifix owned by the Bigallo Museum. Created early in the 13th Century, this Madonna is austere and remote, a reflection of the Byzantine influence. She sits rigidly erect, looking proudly ahead and holding out her Divine Child to be worshiped. But the artist's struggle to depict the figure with a sense of its physical structure, a skill that simply had not been learned by then, and his communication of a feeling of direct contact with the

NATIONAL GALLERY OF ART, WASHINGTON, D.C.

MARGARIT˙ RITIO ME FECIT˙

Margaritone: *Madonna and Child Enthroned,* third quarter of the 13th Century

spectator, mark this painting as unmistakably Italian. Also, a Byzantine artist would rarely have included so mundane a detail as the dots on the Madonna's dress. Margaritone's Madonna *(right),* although it was produced almost 50 years later, is strikingly similar to that of the Bigallo Master. Margaritone was unusual in his time for this reliance on the trusted example of such earlier artists as the Bigallo Master, while his contemporaries were experimenting with more realistic treatments. But Margaritone was confident of his ability—he was one of the first artists to sign his name to his paintings—and he was an extremely popular and quite prolific painter.

St. Peter Master: *St. Peter Altarpiece*, 1275-1285

Florentine School: *St. Michael Altarpiece*, c. mid-13th Century

Having progressed from crucifixes to Madonnas, 13th Century Italian artists began increasingly to devote panels to the lives of the saints. Usually commissioned for churches, chapels or altars dedicated to the saints, these panels often had enlarged narrative side scenes to tell more vividly the subject's life story.

Among the most colorful of the saints was Peter, the leader and spokesman of the Apostles. His life was a fertile source for illustration. For example, in the panel at upper left, painted by an anonymous master, the middle scene at the left shows St. Peter, in a boat with Andrew, being recruited by Christ. The lower right-hand scene pictures his bizarre upside-down crucifixion.

An equally dramatic figure was St. Michael the Archangel *(panel at lower left)*, among whose feats was the conquest of Lucifer, shown in the middle scene on the left. (The ribbons clearly visible alongside St. Michael's head in the central portrayal were an artistic convention of the day, intended to show how the saint's halo was attached.)

Less dramatic but warmer and more poignant is the altar panel depicting Mary Magdalen *(right),* the harlot who became one of Christ's most devoted followers. Flanked by colorful scenes from her life, she is pictured clothed only in her ankle-length hair and holding a scroll that encourages other women to leave the sinful life and "restore yourself to God."

ACCADEMIA, FLORENCE

Magdalen Master: *St. Mary Magdalen Altarpiece,* second half of the 13th Century

SAN FRANCESCO, PESCIA

Bonaventura Berlinghieri: *St. Francis Altarpiece*, 1235

24

St. Francis of Assisi, probably the most popular of all Italian saints, had a profound impact both on Christian thought and art. His life, pictured again and again, reflected a long-forgotten philosophy: that all men are noble and worthy creatures, and that life can be more than a mere rehearsal for death.

One of the earliest representations of St. Francis *(left)* was painted only nine years after his death, too soon to reflect fully the stylistic effects of the saint's humanizing influence. The figures, drawn almost abstractly, are meant mainly to awe the viewer.

Starting at top left, the scenes show Francis at the end of a period of prayer and meditation receiving the stigmata—symbolic wounds representing his identification with Christ—and preaching to the birds, a sign of his communion with God's handiwork (the picture is shown enlarged on this page). Below is the miraculous cure that occurred when a dying child was brought to the saint's tomb. On the right side he is pictured healing persons with withered limbs (also enlarged on this page), healing the lame in prison and exorcising the devil from a madman. Throughout, the emphasis is on the mystical: of the six scenes, four are miracles.

Almost a century later, Giotto would reverse the emphasis: his frescoes in the Bardi Chapel *(pages 144-145),* include only two miracles and stress the saint's personal life.

St. Francis Altarpiece, "St. Francis Talking to the Birds"

St. Francis Altarpiece, "St. Francis Healing the Lame"

The gradual humanization of religious figures by the early 13th Century Italian artists—furthered by the stirring example of St. Francis, a native of their own countryside—reached its climax in the work of Giotto.

Giotto learned much from his predecessors. Like them he did panel paintings—crucifixes, Madonnas, portraits of the saints. But he was searching for a larger expression; his greatest works—narrative tales that seem

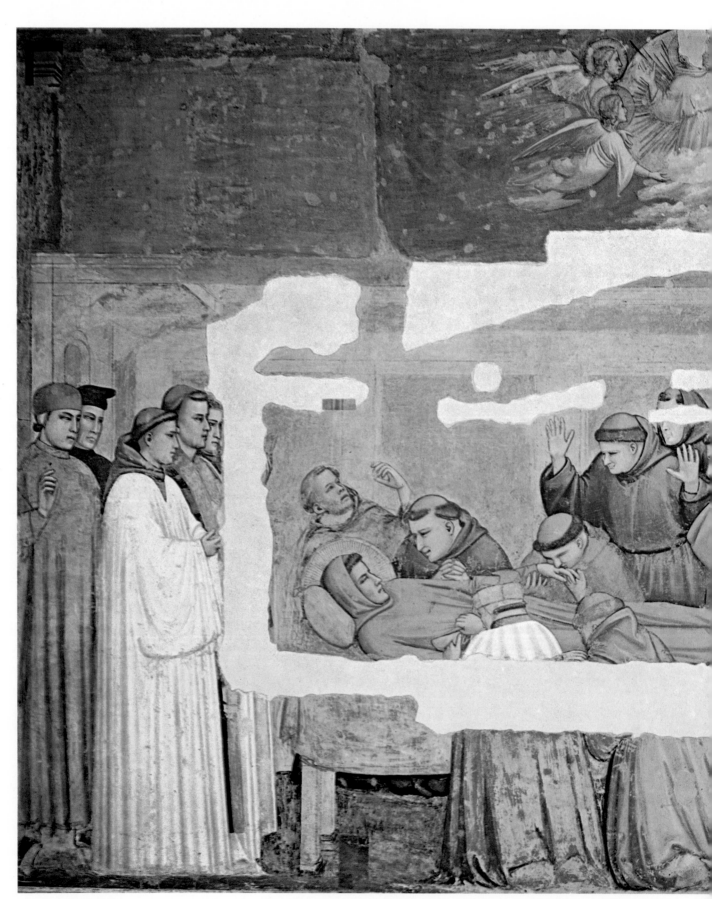

26

almost to burst forth from their confines—were done in fresco, on the walls of churches. In Giotto's work the distant, otherworldly figures of previous painting became warm and human. Giotto's characters, like those clustered around St. Francis in the scene below, are clearly made of flesh and blood, and his drama, too, is a human one: that of a good man dying while his friends and followers grieve.

STA. CROCE, FLORENCE

Bardi Chapel, *The Death of St. Francis,* c. 1315-1320(?)

II

The Painter's Craft

A vivid glimpse of what it was like to be an artist in Giotto's time is provided in a medieval Italian treatise entitled *The Book of Art*. The author, Cennino Cennini, was that rarity, a painter who was also articulate about his craft. Since no known paintings of his survive, his skill with a brush cannot be judged; but his facility with a pen is certain. Cennini's claim to expertise in his field was based on the fact that he had been a pupil of a pupil of a pupil of Giotto's; through this direct link, he asserted, he had absorbed the practical fundamentals of Giotto's craft. Selflessly—as a "labor of love," he put it—he decided to share this lore down to the last detail; in so doing he produced one of the most prized documents in all the annals of art.

Cennini did not see it as his mission to regale his readers with anecdotes handed down from his elders about Giotto, or insights into the great man's personality, or samples of his celebrated wit. He left that to others, and instead dealt intensively with the ordinary workaday problems faced by artists, offering solutions for them that had presumably been employed by Giotto himself.

A reading of Cennini's astonishing medley of recipes, hints, directions and injunctions leads to one inescapable conclusion about the 14th Century Italian who embarked upon a career in art: to stay afloat in his profession, he could not rely upon esthetic inclinations alone. He also had to have the know-how of a carpenter, mason, botanist, geologist, chemist and master chef, the quick reflexes of a trader, a strong back and an ardor for work. One of Cennini's few philosophical asides implored the artist to eat only digestible and wholesome dishes, to drink only light wines, and especially to avoid an excess of female company—a danger, he warned, that causes a painter's hand to "flutter far more than leaves do in the wind."

The ingredients of a work of art are both intangible and tangible. Into its making go such elusive elements as the artist's innate talent and inner vision—and also such mundane materials as pigments and glues and varnishes. In every generation the artist has had to harmonize the esthetic act of painting with the physical act. But vital differences set

This huge Byzantine mosaic adorns the apse of the cathedral at Cefalù, in Sicily. It was made by Greek artists for the Norman King Roger II, under whose benevolent reign Moslem, Jewish, Greek and Roman Catholic cultures lived side by side in peace.

Byzantine mosaic:
Christ Pantocrator, 1148

apart the painters of Giotto's time from those of today. The amount of sheer sweat and toil they had to expend, the ingenuity they had to exercise in the use of tools and techniques, the complications they had to cope with to assemble their materials, all were incomparably greater than at any time since.

A modern painter has but to walk into the nearest art supply store to find a profusion of ready-made aids at his disposal. Chemistry and technology have touched his sphere as all others. With no more exertion than reaching for his wallet, he can acquire canvas stretched to his specifications, boards already primed, swatch books of coordinated color samples, synthetic paints that dry swiftly, and—if he finds the traditional sable or bristle brush too confining—sprays powered by an air turbine or released at the push of a button.

Consider, by contrast, the labors required of Giotto and his contemporaries before they could even begin to paint. They had to cut their own wood panels and build their own frames, make their own brushes and drawing charcoals, grind their own pigments, and concoct their own pastes, sizes, mordants plus all the other mixtures necessary to prepare a painting surface or to affix the paints or to preserve them.

In a world where manufactured products and middlemen's services were new economic notions, the artist often had to go at his task literally from the ground up. Cennini recalled that as a lad he prowled the Tuscan hills looking for natural pigments in the earth, and that at "a very wild steep place, scraping the steep with a spade, I beheld seams of many kinds of color—ocher, dark and light sinoper, blue, and white." It was a practice not restricted to beginners. A century after Cennini, the mighty Michelangelo, seeking suitable reds and yellows for his Sistine Chapel frescoes, took shovel in hand, so the story goes, went down into the Pope's gardens behind the Vatican and, digging into the clay, found the ochers he desired.

Materials other than pigments also had to be sought out and tested, their drawbacks discovered. The knowing painter chose the easy-to-work poplar, linden or willow for his wood panels. For large brushes, he preferred the bristles of a domesticated white hog to those of a wild black hog. He used hard porphyry stone, instead of the softer marble, as a grinding-slab on which to pound and crush the lapis lazuli from which he extracted the most beloved of his colors, ultramarine blue. He drew on his own kitchen for mixing bowls, and exploited such familiar substances as garlic to make his mordants, burnt almond shells to make his blacks, and powdered chicken bones to prime his panels. (Cennini advised taking them "just as you find them under the dining table.")

Cennini did not overtly suggest that economy was an added advantage of these homely stratagems, but he made it plain that a painter had to be as canny as he was inventive. He cautioned his readers to keep a sharp eye out when they went to the apothecary's for one of the pigments they had to obtain by purchase rather than by exploration: vermilion, extracted from cinnabar ore imported from Spain. Always buy vermilion unbroken, not pounded or ground, Cennini counseled, "because it is generally adulterated, either with red lead or with pounded brick." Buying the gold leaf essential to adorn the halos of the Holy Family and the saints also required a wary eye. The gold beaters, Cennini observed, "ought not to get more than a hundred leaves out of a ducat, whereas they do get a hundred and forty-five."

On the other hand, excessively prudent spending could have its disadvantages. Cennini urged the painter not to stint on quality, especially not to try to substitute the less costly golden tin for fine gold when embellishing a work. Anticipating some dissent, he went into his reasons at length. "And if you wish to reply that a poor person cannot make the outlay," he argued, "I answer that if you do your work well, and spend time on your jobs, and good colors, you will get such a reputation that a wealthy person will come to compensate you for the poor one; and your standing will be so good for using good colors that if a master is getting one ducat for a figure, you will be offered two; and you will end by gaining your ambition. As the old saying goes, good work, good pay." By way of afterthought, Cennini offered this consolation: "And even if you were not adequately paid, God and Our Lady will reward you for it, body and soul."

Cennini's undisguised candor would indicate that he intended his words for the eyes only of his fellow craftsmen. But even if inadvertently, the opus he planned as no more than a serviceable handbook also turned out to be a portrait of the medieval artist and his life. It was a life lived at full tilt, busily experimental and boldly competitive. Later centuries would produce the stereotype of the artist as a recluse; in the 1300s and 1400s in Italy, he was concerned with and committed to the swirl of affairs outside his workshop.

He viewed his profession with zest, with pride, and—at least when he had reached the stage where he had journeymen and apprentices to shoulder the physical burdens—with affection even for its difficulties. The story is told that one Sunday afternoon, at the height of his fame, Giotto was chatting with friends on the Via del Cocomero in Florence when a pig broke loose from a passing drove, ran between his legs and knocked him down. Giotto picked himself up, dusted himself off and, to his companions' surprise, smiled fondly. Pigs were pretty smart at that, he commented, and well entitled to take a bit of revenge on him. After all, he explained, "I've earned thousands of *lire* with their bristles, and I've never given them even a dish of swill in return."

The concept of the painter as a special sort of being, subject to his own laws, would have been alien to the Middle Ages. In the strictly structured society of the time everyone had his place, and the painter was no exception. Nor was his place high on the scale. His calling was regarded as a craft, demeaning for scions of the rich or noble but well within the aspirations of an industrious peasant boy or artisan's son.

As a craftsman, the painter had to belong to a guild. In Florence his guild was that of the *Medici e Speziali*—the physicians and his sometime-adversaries across the counter, the apothecaries. However, the artist was hardly on a par with the others. He enjoyed neither the full privileges of membership in the guild nor an active voice in its affairs; he had the subordinate rank of *sottoposto* (literally, "a place below") and only limited control over his own corner of the guild. Even so, his status was loftier than that of the sculptor and architect. His was one of the so-called Greater Guilds, theirs one of the Lesser Guilds; they were lumped with carpenters and bricklayers. It took an extraordinary talent and a forceful personality to hurdle the bounds imposed both by the guild rules and the demands of patrons. Giotto was one of the few who managed this leap. As his mastery of painting became manifest and his reputation grew, he could command a higher price and greater freedom in his work than artists of lesser note.

Dependent upon patronage, the medieval painter hoped and schemed to attract the best sponsors. A bishop in a big town, with the power to assign the decorating of a number of churches, was more to be courted than the prior of one small provincial monastery who might want to pay in farm produce. The ideal secular patron was not just wealthy but socially exalted, hence potentially a trend-setter. But whether churchman or layman, affluent or merely prosperous, the patron held the whip hand over the painter. In an important project, a written contract sealed their arrangements; the painter had to submit to strict specifications as to the size of the work, the colors to be used, the subject matter and sometimes, indeed, the number of figures to be depicted—a primary consideration in computing the fee.

In studying the cycle of St. Francis paintings in Assisi, scholar Millard Meiss and restorer Leonetto Tintori learned a great deal about mural painting techniques, and shed some light on Giotto's disputed authorship of the work. By closely examining the fresco at the right, for example, they were able to identify 21 distinct areas (outlined in white) defined by light cracks and ridges on the plaster surface. Each of these, they reasoned, represented the approximate area of wet plaster a frescoist could paint in one day before it dried. Furthermore, by ascertaining on these joint lines where new plaster overlapped older plaster, they could tell in what order the areas had been painted.

In the 28 St. Francis frescoes, Meiss and Tintori identified 272 areas. Making allowance for humid weather, which enabled artists to work on areas for more than a day, and for the later dry-painting of certain colors and details, they concluded that the cycle had taken longer than a year to complete—and that at least three different masters, not one, must have worked on it.

By custom and convention, the production of heraldic shields, banners for religious processions and for military use, emblems for tourneys and jousts, gilded fabrics all came within the medieval painter's purview. He also decorated caskets and wedding chests and ornamental plates, and provided patterns for carpets. These activities were as much a part of his output as frescoes and panel paintings. Understandably, however, he had preferences. A fresco on a church wall—whether in the nave, transept, side aisles, choir, or chapels—would be seen again and again by hundreds and thousands of worshipers. So would a panel painting placed behind the altar, or hung from the rafters, or attached to the upper part of the choir screen.

These were the roads to renown, riches and, ultimately, to artistic freedom. For as the painter's craft began to turn into an art, frescoes and panel paintings became the major means by which he could express his esthetic intent and demonstrate his technical virtuosity.

Although painting a fresco differs markedly from painting a wood panel, the two techniques held this much in common for their 14th Century practitioner: they required the taking of formidable pains.

In fresco painting, the artist's labors began with the wall on which he was to paint. Since frescoes can survive almost anything but dampness, the inner face of the wall was waterproofed with tar. The wall surface was usually of stone or brick or rubble, textures too rough to be receptive to paint without an intervening layer of thick plaster. Directly on the plaster he would sketch his fresco design in charcoal, and then go over it in red or yellow paint. Then, having assured himself that his design was feasible, he would obliterate the whole thing with *intonaco*—a second finer layer of plaster. Or, as an alternate method—one that came to be preferred—he would apply the intonaco first and the design second.

He was now ready to paint; indeed, he had to be ready. For the whole idea of *buon fresco,* true fresco, was to apply the paint to the plaster while it was still fresh. There was another technique, *fresco secco,* dry fresco, in which the plaster was allowed to dry and then was only slightly dampened before it received the paint; but the paint did not penetrate as well, and the final product was less durable, subject to flaking and peeling. It was for this reason that the other type of fresco was called *buon*—the real thing. For when the paint—a simple mixture of pigment and water—soaked thoroughly into the wet plaster, the lime in the plaster acted as a chemical binder. As a result, the paint became an integral, permanent part of the plaster.

This chemical reality ruled the painter's entire procedure, engaging him in a race with time, a contest in which he pitted his swiftness and sureness of hand against the speed with which the plaster dried.

Many a fresco artist learned the hard way. He would cover a large area of wall with his intonaco and design, and proceed to paint—only to find at day's end that sizable sections of intonaco still remained to be painted. The next day he had to cut away these sections, which had hardened inexorably overnight, mix and apply a new batch of wet plaster and re-apply his design before he could start to paint anew. In time, the artist reduced the hazard to a minimum by applying the intonaco only to as much wall surface as he was sure he could paint in one session.

Painting a wood panel also offered its challenges—despite Cennini's assertion that it was "the nicest and the neatest occupation that we have in our profession. . ." But preparing the surface was no less essential than in fresco work, for if the artist applied his paints directly to the wood the resins in it would eventually discolor them. First he planed his board—selected from lumber as free as possible of grain and knots—to a satiny smoothness. Next he sealed the surface with a weak solution of size, a glutinous wash that filled the wood pores and provided an adhesive base. Cennini's suggested recipe for a suitable size was one made of water and boiled-down parchment clippings—a combination that he claimed gave the wood as much of a taste for later coatings "as if you were fasting, and ate a handful of sweetmeats, and drank a glass of good wine, which is an inducement for you to eat your dinner."

The menu in store for the wood was an extensive one. Over the size the painter placed strips of white linen, over the linen a coating of gesso (pulverized chalk mixed with glue) and over the gessoed cloth—the forerunner of the canvas used by later painters—layer after layer of finer gesso until it had been built up to a desired thickness. Once dry, the surface would be scraped smooth. If the proposed painting was large—an increasing likelihood as bigger churches were built and bigger altarpieces were ordered to adorn them—several boards were glued together.

Other steps had to be taken before painting. The design, worked out in preliminary sketches, was drawn on the gesso. Sometimes this was done with charcoal, and sometimes by covering the back of the drawing with lampblack, laying it against the gesso, and retracing the outline to create an imprint.

If the artist planned a gold background, he might have to cover the gesso with as many as 10 coats of a special variety of size—made of red clay—to hold the extremely fragile gold leaf. Ever mindful of his costs, the painter would coat the entire surface with the leaf only if the panel was small; if it was big, he would lay the leaf around the figures or scenes to be painted.

After the burnishing of the leaf came, at last, the painting. The simple watercolors of fresco would not stick to gesso. Some binding material had to be added, and far and away the painter's favorite was the lowly egg—the yolk alone or together with some white. Using egg tempera—the blend of pigment and water and egg—he proceeded with his ultimate task. This in itself required consummate care; if only a few coats of color were applied, they would not show over white gesso; as many as 30 coats might be needed. Then, since tempera dries to a dull finish, the painter would apply varnish or polish the surface with beeswax.

As a matter of course, the painter would relegate to his assistants most of the tedious, time-consuming chores involved in preparing both panels and frescoes. Even in the final execution of the work he often permitted his more seasoned helpers to paint everything but the heads and major figures. But one area of responsibility was his alone: the determination of the style he would employ.

Few medieval Italian painters were very adventurous; Giotto was without peer in his ability and willingness to innovate. The majority avoided a quest for new frontiers. They derived their ideas from styles of the past—the Classical, the Byzantine, the Romanesque—and from the new Gothic style as well. Most of them were, however, far from slavish copyists. They could not be, for these styles were often expressed not in frescoes or panels but in other forms which had to be translated and adapted to the painting medium. A bas-relief on the side of an antique marble sarcophagus might teach the painter the elements of the Classical style; he might glean his understanding of the Byzantine from mosaics, of the Romanesque from carved reliefs, and of the Gothic from the statues on church portals.

The Classical and the Romanesque were part of Italy's own heritage. Moreover, all four styles appeared in small-scale form in illuminated manuscripts, carved ivories, enameled plaques, or portable altarpieces and other personal devotional objects. The untutored observer might merely admire these diminutive works; the knowledgeable painter could discern in them their stylistic essence—the treatment of the human form and its draperies, the use of decorative motifs, as well as the general rhythm and harmony of the composition.

The most venerable of the styles, the Classical—more than a thousand years old by Giotto's time—had originated in Greece, and had later been taken over by the conquering Romans. Reflecting the Greeks' preoccupation with physical beauty and the joys of the here-and-now, the hallmark of the Classical was the nude human figure, natural in its proportions but highly idealized. When draperies were depicted, they were made to cling to the body to accentuate it. Nothing was permitted to detract from the figure's importance. When a background was used, as in a relief sculpture, it was scrupulously plain. The composition as a whole was simple and symmetrical, in keeping with the Greek love of the rational and the well-ordered.

The Byzantine style retained only the balanced composition of the Classical. Three-dimensional figures gave way to two-dimensional figures, entirely unspecific as to anatomical detail, austerely frontal in their pose, with large staring eyes—focused elsewhere than on terrestrial matters. Draperies did not emphasize the figure; instead, they served to provide rhythmic effects. The gold background that was a staple also had its purpose: to turn the viewer's thoughts from his earthly environs to the wondrous supernatural world beyond.

Byzantine art, in sum, reflected the fact that the Byzantine Empire was a Christian theocracy of the most rigorous sort. Like all other enterprise, the artist's craft was subservient to the purposes of church and state. The artist well knew that his function was not to express his individuality but to produce visualizations of Christian dogma: works that would, at one and the same time, instruct and overwhelm the viewer. Matters of style were directly related to Christianity's concern with the otherworldly. Facing a life hereafter, the believer had no reason to be distracted with the things of this world, including the transient beauty of mortal flesh.

So well did the Byzantine artist do his appointed work that the very images, or icons, that he produced began to be worshiped in themselves, and therein lay deep trouble. Ultimately the widespread belief that the icons had supernatural powers and could perform miracles caused a major crisis throughout the Byzantine Empire. Ranged against the icon-worshipers were those who insisted that the adoration of holy images was pagan. This anti-icon point of view prevailed for much of the Eighth Century and part of the Ninth; the so-called iconoclasts, or icon-smashers, indulged in a wholesale destruction of works of art.

Then a halt was called, although artists continued to work under strict limitations. Their scope was defined by a pronouncement of a church council at Nicaea: "The composition of the figures is not the invention of the painters but the law and tradition of the Church, and this purpose and tradition is not the part of the painter (for his is only the art) but is due to the ordination and the disposition of our Fathers."

The theologians' decrees governed not only the artist's range of subject matter—restricting it largely to depictions of Christ, the Virgin, the saints, apostles, and prophets, Scriptural episodes and scenes of major feast days—but also the attributes and gestures of the figures. This limitation might have made the artist's efforts wholly predictable and his art static except for a crucial fact of geography: Byzantium's proximity to the cultures of the East. In their art, the Persians and other Eastern peoples made rich use of bright colors and decorative motifs. The Byzantine artist took over these features, recognizing in them the avenues to self-expression otherwise denied him. How well he succeeded is seen in his most spectacular legacy, the great mosaics on the domes and vaults and walls of Byzantine churches. It is their color and their rhythmically repeated abstract patterns that first impress the viewer, together creating a hypnotic effect that few forms of art have surpassed.

While Byzantine art was flourishing anew, Romanesque art—also dedicated to the service of the Church—began to emerge in Western Europe, taking different forms in different localities. The Romanesque acquired its name by borrowing structural ideas from Roman monuments still extant. But this heritage from the Classical showed up primarily in Romanesque church architecture, in its heavy columns, rounded arches and solid mass. Romanesque painting drew inspiration from the Byzantine—from illuminated manuscripts and carved ivories circulated among monasteries, and also from painted icons.

Along with these borrowed features the Romanesque absorbed the native art of Europe's barbarian tribes. Originally a carver's craft expressed in ornaments found on buckles, brooches, daggers and horse-trappings, this art was unconcerned with reproducing the human figure. It was, however, fascinated with animals—more often imagined than real—and with intricately interwoven designs. Applying this busy quality to the depiction of human forms, the Romanesque evolved its own stylistic synthesis. The forms were still two-dimensional, as in the Byzantine figures, but usually exaggerated, distorted, either squat and stunted or grotesquely elongated. For all this they had a great deal of fluid grace. Draperies swirled around and away from the body in restless sweeps. The entire composition generated a sense of vitality, move-

In the Eighth Century, Byzantine emperors proscribed the use of icons, believing that their subjects were worshiping these religious images with idolatrous zeal; the manuscript illumination above shows an iconoclast, or icon-destroyer, acting under imperial orders, as he whitewashes a painted Christ. Forbidden to create such works, and persecuted in a struggle between state and church, many artistically skilled monks left Byzantium for the more hospitable climate of Italy, bringing a fresh infusion of the Byzantine style.

ment, dynamism. It was an art well suited to the physical violence, the religious fervor, the general turbulence of its time.

Toward the first half of the 12th Century a new style appeared, initially in Northern France, that would eventually edge out the Romanesque. This was Gothic, and originally it, too, was a Church art, most resplendently realized in cathedral architecture; one of its unique structural features, the pointed arch, would be adapted by Giotto and his colleagues in the thrones they painted. But an element of Gothic style more intriguing to the painters was the treatment of the human form, notably in the sculpture adorning the cathedrals. The Gothic figure had the naturalism of the Classical figure, with an all-important difference. In place of the glorification of the body in all its muscular nudity, the Gothic representation concentrated on a faithful rendering of the face and the hands. The figure was covered by draperies that enhanced its shape without explicitly showing it.

Gothic sculptors were undertaking to translate into visual images in stone the idea that Christianity must speak to men in their own terms—a concept that Giotto would later translate into visual images in paint. They concentrated on the hands and faces of their figures because these were vehicles of human expressiveness. By carving a smile on the Virgin's lips, inclining her head toward her Son, forming her fingers into a caressing gesture, they could turn her from a forbidding vision of sovereignty into a tender likeness of motherhood. Draperies, too, could be useful, underscoring the emotion the artist wished to convey by the way they were bunched, by the turns they were made to take—subtle directional arrows, as it were, encouraging the viewer to comprehend.

Of the styles available to the medieval Italian painter, the Byzantine was the most influential. As far back as the Sixth Century, Justinian, the Byzantine Emperor, had appointed an exarch, or viceroy, to govern parts of Italy from Ravenna, on Italy's Adriatic shores, and had also brought the southern part of the country under his control—a rule that was to last until the Norman conquests 500 years later. Many of the churches and monasteries built in these areas were decorated by craftsmen and artists imported from Constantinople. Some of these men also migrated on their own, refugees from the wrath of the iconoclasts.

The influx of Byzantine art left its marks all along the Italian peninsula; some are visible today in the mosaics of the churches of San Vitale in Ravenna, San Marco in Venice, and Monreale in Sicily. The native painter who did not see such works at first hand had other ways of acquainting himself with the products of Byzantine style: through the regular channels of trade with Constantinople and through the sometimes irregular channels of Crusades.

Ostensibly, the Crusades had been launched to recover the Holy Land from the infidels, but they had political, evangelistic and materialistic purposes as well. One chronicler observed that "some went to the East out of curiosity; others, who had lived at home in pinching poverty, wanted only to fight . . . in order to end their poverty; still others fled from their debts, from duties which they ought to have performed, or from punishments which their crimes had deserved. Only a few could be found who did not bow their knees unto Baal, and who were actuated by a holy purpose." Beginning in 1095, three campaigns had been sent out from Western Europe. They had been largely unsuccessful in their main goal, but a quantity of art, gold and other treasures had found its way back home. When Pope Innocent III was elected in 1198, one of his first acts was to sanction a Fourth Crusade. The original plan was to set up a military base in Egypt from which an attack against the Mohammedans could be mounted. But Innocent's Crusaders, drawn from a variety of European kingdoms, needed help. Lacking transportation, they turned to the republic of Venice, whose powerful fleet strove constantly for trade dominance in the Mediterranean.

After a complicated and expensive series of negotiations, the expedition set sail—not for Egypt, as the Crusaders had originally intended, but for Constantinople, toward which Venice had craftily redirected the mission. On April 13, 1204, after several sieges, the ancient city fell to the Crusaders. Promptly there ensued what has often been described as one of the blackest chapters in European history. The Crusaders ruthlessly sacked a community whose cultural heritage derived in an unbroken line from the ancient Greeks and which was, moreover, as Christian as Rome itself. A priceless treasury of ancient literature and art was either destroyed on the spot or carried off to be ruined or mutilated later. An eyewitness, indeed one of the Crusade leaders, disgusted by the lawlessness, wrote: "The booty gained was so great that none could tell you the end of it; gold and silver and vessels and precious stones and samite and cloth of silver and robes . . . ermine and every choicest thing found upon the earth." Guided by the Venetians, who knew the city intimately from having traded there, the looters carried off statuary, illuminated manuscripts, miniatures and mosaic and precious ivory. Directly to Venice came four huge bronze horses, which were set up in the Piazza di San Marco, and the gold-and-enamel and jeweled plaques that together became the *Pala d'Oro,* the magnificent altarpiece of the church of San Marco. Thus, by foul means and fair, the Byzantine style had become a familiar presence in Italian art by the time of the 13th Century. The efforts of Italian painters of that era were frankly derivative. Much, of course, depended on the individual's own talent and perceptivity. Some works were little more than routine copies of the Byzantine; some showed freshness and intimations of a new power.

On a wall of the Museo Nazionale in Pisa hangs a panel painting, cruciform in shape, which, because of its numerical listing in the museum catalogue, has come to be called the *Pisa No. 20 Crucifix (page 19).* It is a considerably larger crucifix than those of earlier centuries—nearly 10 feet high and almost 7 feet at its widest. The size alone is noteworthy, reflecting the grander needs of grander churches that were abuilding in the 13th Century. The painting is not on the gesso of later panels but on purple vellum affixed to the wood. Christ is shown on the Cross; at His right hand are the Virgin and St. John, at His left the two Marys; above Him is a scene of the Ascension and below a scene of the Descent into Hell. Flanking His sides are six other small scenes, depicting episodes after the Crucifixion.

In his choice of subject, the painter was treading a path worn by countless Christian artists before him, of various centuries, regions and styles. But in his treatment he was decidedly Byzantine. He depicted Christ not as the Romanesque artist had done—head erect, eyes open, triumphant over death—but in the manner of Byzantine crucifixions, in which Christ was represented as dead, eyes closed, head slumped on shoulder. The six scenes at Christ's sides have the involved symbolism dear to Byzantine doctrine, the elegant orderliness of its art, its pronounced rhythm and pattern. The richness of the purple vellum is embellished with an abundance of gold leaf. The painter of *Pisa No. 20* had not only studied his lessons but mastered them.

Another panel painting of the same period—about the second quarter of the 13th Century—displays a significant progression from the *Pisa No. 20 Crucifix*. This work—the *Madonna Enthroned (page 20)*—is only about two by three feet in size, and rectangular in shape, broken only by the protrusion of the Virgin's halo at the top. She sits aloof and abstracted. Her throne is entirely without substance—not a seat but merely an appropriate symbol to be set beneath the Queen of Heaven. The Christ Child does not sit in her lap; He is merely placed against her chest. He is not a baby but ageless, completely removed from so worldly a concept as time.

Thus far, this painting is thoroughly Byzantine. But there are small details, still only slight, of the kind that presage the onset of artistic change. With the most tentative delicacy, the Madonna's fingers just touch the Child's feet. A Byzantine painter would not have dared to depict the Madonna holding the Child in a firm grip. But the painter of this work was an Italian. When he showed the Madonna touching her Child, however lightly, he was showing the first trace of the revolt that was to occur against the spirituality of Byzantium—the first sign of an independent Italian style of painting in which physical contact, bulk, solidity, would be basic features.

The draperies that swathe the Madonna in a sweep of loose blue folds, obscuring the outline of her body, making her look less like a mortal woman, were also a Byzantine influence. But at the same time the painter decorated the skirt with a pattern of dots. Lavish as they were with color and design, the artists of Byzantium would never have permitted themselves so frivolous a decoration: that would have been too much like an article from a woman's wardrobe—a decoration not only too secular but positively irreverent. To the Italians, the Queen of Heaven was to become fully a woman, wearing both the expression and the garments of a woman. So, in the dotted fabric, the painter took a tentative step away from Byzantine absolutism toward Italian humanism.

Because a crucifix believed to be by the same artist now hangs in the Bigallo Museum in Florence, the painter of this *Madonna Enthroned* is called the Bigallo Master. His real identity is lost, as is the name of the painter of the *Pisa No. 20 Crucifix*. Until about the middle of the 13th Century, anonymity was to be the fate of most artists; if they labored to win immortality for their names, almost all labored in vain. In this respect, too, Italian art was soon to change.

A Meeting of Styles

By the time of Giotto's birth, four different styles —Byzantine, Romanesque, Gothic and Classical—had interacted in Italy to give art a broad new range of expression. Since Italy was an aggressive trading center and the seat of the Western Church, works of art in various styles flowed into its cities as items of commerce, as booty from military conquests and Crusades, and as gifts to the Popes. Foreign kings with territories in Italy also introduced their native art. Thus, Italian artists knew many influences, which they combined with their own ideas and expressed in many individual forms.

The Classical style, with its man-centered imagery, was native to Italy, having grown out of the Roman inheritance of the Greek tradition. The Byzantine style —familiar to Italians in reliefs like the one shown at right—was imported from the East; its austere depiction of figures stressed spiritual values. Romanesque art, a blending of the Classicism brought north by Roman legions with a native Northern European art, abounded in geometric, animal and floral motifs. The Gothic style, French in origin, was distinguished by more realistic, mobile, and expressive figures. The development and interplay of these styles can be seen clearly in the work of outstanding Italian sculptors of the period—work that, because of its public character, exerted a constant influence on other sculptors and painters of the day.

Small, portable art works, like this commemorative ivory relief, which shows Christ conferring power on an emperor and his consort, taught Italian artists much about the art of other cultures. The rigid, formal treatment of the figures is characteristic of the Byzantine style.

Coronation of Romanos and Eudoxia, c. 950

CATHEDRAL OF SANTA MARIA ASSUNTA, PARMA

Benedetto Antelami: *The Deposition*, 1178

The Romanesque style, largely a product of German and French artists, appeared in Northern Italy early in the 12th Century. Among those who adopted the style was Benedetto Antelami, who carved this stunning marble relief in 1178, adding his name and the date in a lettered band that runs across the panel above the arms of the Cross—an indication of his self-confidence and his renown.

The scene, originally carved to adorn a pulpit or altar screen, depicts the lowering of Christ from the Cross. Nicodemus, on the ladder, removes the nail from His left hand. The wealthy Jew who was a secret disciple of Christ, Joseph of Arimathea (shown in the detail at right), kisses His wound as he lifts the body down; the Virgin sorrowfully presses His right hand to her face. At the right of the scene, four Roman soldiers cast lots for the prize of Christ's robe.

Restrained though the composition may appear, it reveals an underlying dramatic tension typical of the Romanesque style. For example, Antelami has conveyed the spiritual agitation of the mourners at the left by the many rippling folds of their garments and their strained, anguished glances.

Anon.: *Isaiah (left)* and *Ezekiel (right)*, first half of 12th Centu

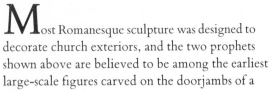

Most Romanesque sculpture was designed to decorate church exteriors, and the two prophets shown above are believed to be among the earliest large-scale figures carved on the doorjambs of a

European cathedral. Flat and frontal, they are clearly part of the architecture, seeming to be confined within the stone block from which they were sculpted. Their vitality comes largely from surface decoration, particularly

CATHEDRAL OF STA. MARIA AND S. BASSIANO, LODI

Anon.: *Eve (left)* and *Adam (right)*, second half of 12th Century

from the linear patterns of robes, beards and hair.

The Adam and Eve above, carved by another anonymous sculptor, show other conventions of the Romanesque style: the cross-legged poses, the curves of the bodies, the circular folds of the drapery, the inclinations of the heads. But a humanization has occurred here that would continue to develop in Italian art until it finally came into full flower in the Renaissance.

45

BAPTISTERY, PISA

Nicola Pisano: Pulpit, 1260

Ancient Roman sculpture, and Roman copies of Greek sculpture, abounded in Italy and had long served as models for local artists. Among the greatest 13th Century inheritors of this Classical tradition was Nicola Pisano, whose earliest known work is the pulpit shown here. One of its relief panels *(below)* contains, in a space less than four feet wide, three Biblical episodes pertaining to Christ's birth; in the upper left corner is the Annunciation (also shown in detail on the opposite page); at the center is the Nativity and at the right is the Annunciation to the Shepherds.

The style of the panel is plainly Classical, as can be seen from the proportions and toga-like drapery of the figures, the staid reclining pose of the Virgin—which makes her look something like a Roman matron—and the curly beard of Joseph *(lower left corner)*. Also, Nicola's use of a building cornice in the background is a familiar Classical device for heightening the illusion of depth. But his architectural design for the pulpit itself includes some unusual departures: the hexagonal shape, the columns between panels and the tracery in the arches are hints of Gothic motifs. Although the total impression of his own work is that of a Classicist, Nicola's introduction of these elements foreshadows a still greater synthesis of styles in later Italian art.

The Gothic style achieved its most dynamic expression in Italian sculpture in the hands of Giovanni Pisano, son of the classically oriented Nicola, in whose workshop the young artist had been trained. Like his father's pulpit, shown on the preceding page, Giovanni's pulpit for the cathedral at Pistoia *(left)* is hexagonal in plan and supported by seven foliated columns, but the arches are now pointed in a more purely Gothic manner.

The most striking contrast with Nicola's restrained Classicism, however, is Giovanni's treatment of movement and human forms. His Nativity scene *(below)* fairly throbs with action and emotion: the announcing angel, shown in the detail at right, joyously approaches the shy, unbelieving Mary; the reclining Madonna protectively covers her newborn Son, and the women in the foreground bustle about preparing for the Child's bath. Giovanni carved the relief deeply to emphasize the feeling of motion; some of the figures on the pulpit stand out a full eight inches from the background. He further heightened the effect of depth by coloring the background areas and some parts of the figures, a common device on such reliefs. The result of these techniques—a combination of Giovanni's own Italian vitality and the Gothic style that he adopted—is a work that teems with life.

Giovanni Pisano: Pulpit, 1301

The most dramatic panel from Giovanni's Pistoia pulpit is the one depicting King Herod's barbaric slaughter of innocent children in a frantic effort to destroy the newborn Christ. Here, Giovanni emphasizes the tumultuous action and the frenzied mood of the scene by abandoning finely chiseled details and concentrating on

Giovanni Pisano: *Massacre of the Innocents*, 1301

deeply cut, almost cubic forms. Faces and bodies are strained and taut as the terrified mothers try to flee with their babies from the murdering soldiers under the imperious command of Herod *(upper right)*. In this powerful scene, Giovanni fully exploited the emotional and expressive possibilities of the Gothic style.

SAN DOMENICO, ORVIETO

Arnolfo di Cambio: Monument to Cardinal Guillaume de Braye, 1282.

A successful fusion of the Gothic and Classical styles was achieved by Arnolfo di Cambio, a former student of Nicola Pisano who became one of Italy's leading architects and the designer of Florence's great Cathedral, the Duomo. Among his first major commissions was a tomb for the French Cardinal Guillaume de Braye, who died in 1282 while visiting Pope Martin IV in Orvieto. Arnolfo's plan included a Gothic-arched tabernacle to surround the tomb, but during the 17th Century the entire structure was moved and the tabernacle was destroyed. The elements that remain are the sarcophagus, with an effigy of the Cardinal; niches contain carved figures of St. Dominic *(right),* founder of the order to which the Cardinal belonged, and St. Mark presenting a kneeling de Braye *(left)* to the Virgin and Child *(top).*

In his designs for the tomb, Arnolfo followed the practice of Rome's leading monument makers, the Cosmati, in decorating his surfaces with brightly colored marble inlays and glass mosaic. But he asserted his own sculptural style in the carved figures, especially the two acolytes who draw aside the curtains of the Cardinal's sepulcher (detail at right). Throughout his works, Arnolfo's adroit placement of forms and his sturdy, full-bodied figures encourage the belief that painters —including Giotto, who is thought to have been his good friend—learned a great deal from him.

GALLERIA DEGLI UFFIZI, FLORENCE

III

Ferment in
Tuscany

The largest Madonna of its time—
almost 15 feet tall and 9½ feet wide—
this panel painting by the Sienese
master Duccio was designed for
a Florentine church. Influenced by the
sinuous and expressive French Gothic
style, Duccio pictured the Virgin
with a fluid silhouette, tenderly
supporting her Child and receiving
the adoring glances of angels.

Duccio: *Rucellai Madonna*, 1285

Sometime during the 13th Century, painting in Italy took a turn that
was to set the course of Western art for 600 years. The change came
subtly; but by the last third of the century it was noticeable. Painting,
although still very much a craft, began to be seen as an art as well. Separate schools developed, each with its distinctive stamp. And out of the
faceless mass of artists men arose—Giotto preeminently among them—
whose talents would perpetuate their names.

Never noted for its calm, Italy in the 13th Century was one vast hub-
bub of battle. Popes and emperors warred for sovereignty, princes for
realms, cities for trading advantage. Almost every locality had its feuds
and alignments: clan versus clan, noble versus commoner, upper versus
lower bourgeois, the laboring poor versus them all. Seething enmities
awaited only a spark to erupt. The century's worst carnage, the Sicilian
Vespers of 1282, in which the islanders rose up and slew a French occu-
pying force of several thousand men, was touched off by a soldier's pur-
ported insult to a local belle.

Yet along with the strife there was striving; with the violence, vigor;
and with the bloodthirstiness, a taste for beauty. In the midst of tumult,
Italians looked around them and decided that their cities needed adorn-
ment. The artist, like the fighting man, became an instrument of civic
pride, a weapon in rivalries that began to be cultural as well as political.

In all of Italy the drive to beautify was strongest in the region of Tuscany, and especially in the Tuscan cities of Lucca, Pisa, Siena and Florence. The lead they took was so great that for a long time afterward
Italian art was essentially Tuscan art, and what evolved as the Italian
Renaissance was largely a Tuscan achievement. The Lucchese and Pisans, the Sienese and Florentines were as often foes as friends. They
fought and bullied and betrayed one another regularly. Each city had
its own qualities. But Tuscany itself seemed more than just the sum of
its parts: a separate entity, with a special character and flavor and verve.
In this phenomenon, perhaps, lay the secret of its ascendancy.

The complexities of the Tuscan mystique still baffle its devotees. Some
credit the Tuscans' confident ways to their descent from the gifted Etrus-

cans of archaic time. Some ascribe their esthetic sense simply to their surroundings: from the Apennines on the east to the Tyrrhenian Sea on the west, along the Arno and its tributaries, on every ridge and plain, the vista pleases, and cries out to be painted.

An appraisal that may come closest to the mark was made in the 20th Century by the author Curzio Malaparte. In a book entitled *Those Cursed Tuscans,* he listed some of the singularities that their countrymen might try to emulate. "Learn from the Tuscans," he wrote, "how to spit in the face of the mighty, in the face of kings, emperors, bishops, inquisitors, judges, masters, adulators of every kind. . . . Learn from the Tuscans that there is nothing sacred in this world except the human himself, and that one human's soul is worth precisely that of another's: and that it is only necessary to know how to keep the soul clean. . . . The Tuscans, who are frightfully jealous of their souls, know how to keep them clean: and woe unto him who tries to dirty that soul, or humiliate it, or butter it up, or bless it, mortgage it, rent it, buy it."

"Without Tuscany," Malaparte claimed, "Italy would be only a piece of Europe." This is not a statement to be taken lying down by partisans of other corners of the peninsula. But at least insofar as it applies to 13th Century art, it stirs little debate.

W hoever defined history as just a confused heap of facts may well have had Tuscan history in mind. One of the facts about it that comes through clearly, however, is that a woman's recalcitrance helped launch the Tuscans on their upward march. Possibly because she was more capable than seductive, posterity remembers her less than queens and paramours who shaped events by their charms alone. Her name was Countess Matilda—*la gran contessa,* the people called her—and she dominated Tuscany for almost 50 years, from the late 11th Century to the early 12th.

To understand Matilda's role it is necessary to glance at an earlier era. After the death of Charlemagne, who gave Europe its first unified regime since the Caesars, his empire was split into three parts, roughly corresponding to modern France, Germany and Northern Italy. In the next century the vision of empire recurred to a forceful German King, Otto the Great. In 961 he crossed the Alps and took over Northern Italy and Tuscany. In Rome, the Pope was beset by enemies. He asked and got Otto's help, and in gratitude crowned him—as a previous Pope had crowned Charlemagne—"Emperor Ever August of the Romans."

The effects were to plague Europe interminably. The initial harmony between popes and emperors turned to distrust, contention over prerogatives, and outright combat. The expanded domain of Otto and his heirs —the Holy Roman Empire, as it became known—was doomed to instability. As a safeguard, the emperors arranged to have their Italian holdings run by local lords who, in return for the feudal vows of allegiance, were given a free hand over their areas. In Tuscany in 1027 this plum fell to Matilda's father. After a long and rapacious rule he was assassinated, and Matilda, as his only surviving child, succeeded him.

It is remarkable enough that, in an age where women were expected to defer to their male betters, Matilda would don helmet and armor and lead her troops in the field. But she also flouted a sterner tradition. Heed-

Italian maritime republics and inland city-states grew rich from the traffic of Crusaders who used the peninsula's main roads *(dark lines on map)* and ports on their way from Western Europe to the Near East in the 12th and 13th Centuries. These centers traded with, plotted against and warred on one another to gain commercial dominance. They also competed for the services of artists; Giotto traveled as far north as Milan and as far south as Naples to execute commissions.

less of her feudal obligations, she chose to side with the popes in their deepening quarrels with the emperors.

Matilda was conspicuously devout; one theory has it that she turned to religion after a brief, ill-starred union with a warrior famed as Godfrey the Hunchback, Duke of Lower Lorraine. In any event, she became an outspoken ally of the Church. Indeed, the most dramatic confrontation in Church annals—between Pope Gregory VII and Emperor Henry IV—took place at her castle at Canossa in 1077. Henry had taken to naming his own bishops and, moreover, to conferring on them the ring and the crozier that were the emblems of their spiritual authority. For a layman to perform this solemn symbolic act of investiture was, to the Church, unthinkable. Gregory set out for Germany to consider Henry's ouster, and en route stopped over at Canossa. Learning of the mission, Henry decided to repent. He rushed south and stood, abject and barefoot, in the snows at Canossa's gates. After three days the Pope pardoned him. But the triumph of church over state was transitory. Henry was young and resilient, and he soon renewed the investiture struggle.

It was now that Matilda rendered the first of her services to Tuscany's future. Although Henry urged her to support him against the Pope—alternately cajoling and threatening, and even attacking Canossa—she refused to yield her convictions. The rift between countess and overlord widened beyond repair. The people of Tuscany knew an opening when they saw it. Correctly concluding that the protagonists would need and seek their support, they put a price on it: freedom in their local affairs.

By trading and seafaring, the Tuscan towns had put on economic muscle; by nibbling away at the authority of their feudal masters, they had also gained control of some simple municipal functions. But they wanted a lot more latitude and, above all, the stamp of legality. In return for their money and manpower, Henry assented—although not without some bargaining finesse. In 1081 he granted Pisa, the richest of the towns, a charter that made it virtually independent. The same year he gave Lucca a charter with substantial rights and privileges. Siena, less affluent, got no formal upgrading, but was at least not deterred from electing its own spokesmen. Florence could expect nothing from Henry. Long Matilda's favorite, it continued to stand at her side. Whether out of gratitude or necessity, she looked the other way when the Florentines began collecting their own taxes and wrecking the castles of rural nobles who tried to hold up their traders.

Matilda's benefactions to Tuscany were not yet done. Dying childless, she left her immense properties to be fought over by emperor and pope; this she achieved by deciding that only her feudal lands should revert to the emperor, while her inherited family lands should go to the Church. In the resulting imbroglio the Tuscan towns again profited, seizing great chunks of the disputed countryside beyond their walls. They now had elbow room as well as economic and political heft. Henceforth, despite occasional setbacks, they kept gaining ground in all directions. By the 13th Century, they had become aggressive city-states, flourishing, self-assured and ready to enjoy the amenities of life.

In this buoyant climate the artist, too, displayed a new confidence,

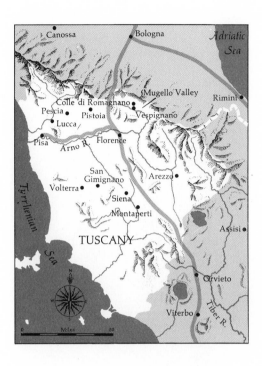

Tuscany, Giotto's home region—both Colle di Romagnano and Vespignano claim to be his birthplace—emerged as the financial and artistic center of Italy in the 13th Century. Its principal cities—Florence, Siena, Lucca, Arezzo, Volterra and Pisa—vied with one another until Florence, dominating the trade routes *(dark lines)*, triumphed. When the rising middle class gained control of the city in 1267, the year of Giotto's birth, the supremacy of mercantile Florence was assured.

an urge to venture. To be sure, his venturings were highly tentative; he had no wish to renounce religious subject matter or abandon his old Byzantine guidelines of style. Byzantine art was, in fact, providing a fresh fount of ideas: after Constantinople was laid waste in the Fourth Crusade in 1204, its artists began to revitalize their tradition, painting with freer brushstrokes and giving a sense of movement and substance to figures once fixed and two-dimensional.

The Tuscan painters benefited by the Byzantine Renaissance, but they also set out on a search for their own identity. The day of ringing artistic manifestoes was still far distant, and the artists' quest was never openly proclaimed. Instead, it took the form of random probings in particular works—a quick foray into the experimental, a small departure from established convention. Gradually these innovations took hold. Together, they came to represent a style of painting that was no longer Italo-Byzantine but clearly and recognizably Italian.

It was a style well suited to a people with a flair for theatrics. For the Tuscan artist, merely to depict the Madonna or the crucified Christ or a cherished saint was not enough. He surrounded his central figures with all sorts of episodic scenes; while storytelling in paint was not new, he reveled in it. He had ample material to work with, both from Scripture and from the mass of apocryphal legend subsequently added to it. But whatever the subject, he organized his scenes with the care of an impresario. He arranged his figures purposefully and emphasized this placement by rhythmic accents that governed even the direction of glances. The total effect was that of a play being enacted upon a stage.

The play, however, had lifelike overtones. Conscious of his spectators, the painter filled his scenes with reminders of the realities they knew. Real people and objects were physical and tangible; his people touched each other, rested a hand on a table or chair. Real people existed in three dimensions; he confirmed the existence of the dimensions by shadings that made objects seem to recede, giving an illusion of depth. Real faces wore varied expressions and so did those he painted. He was a long way from a mastery of space or tactility or the gamut of emotions. But he had made a start, and out of his small-scale testing ground came the ordered drama, the rhythmic sweep, and the lively, earthy qualities that later marked the most monumental Italian masterworks.

It remained for Giotto to come along and infuse painting with the special strain of genius that makes him rightfully regarded as the grandfather of Italian art. Still, even grandfathers have forebears, and in the decades prior to his rise other artists imprinted their names on their own times and thereafter.

Every major Tuscan city boasted its resident talents. Lucca had a whole family of painters—the Berlinghieri, father and three sons, of whom Bonaventura is best remembered. Pisa had Giunta Pisano, Florence had Coppo di Marcovaldo, Siena had Guido da Siena; there were others besides, in these places and elsewhere. The era had not yet arrived when biographers would analyze artistic personalities, and virtually nothing is known of these men as individuals. An occasional surviving document sheds a faint ray on some detail of their lives: for example, that

VATICAN LIBRARY, ROME

This manuscript illumination shows Henry IV, the powerful German Emperor, kneeling before Matilda, the great countess of Tuscany, and Abbot Hugh of Cluny, Pope Gregory VII's spokesman. Henry had been excommunicated for usurping the papal privilege of naming bishops and abbots. To restore himself to the Church he sought out the Pope, who was staying at Matilda's castle in the Apennine Mountains. As a humiliation, Gregory left Henry standing barefoot in the snow for three days before he relented.

the Berlinghieri were among the citizens of Lucca who signed a peace pact with Pisa in 1228, and that Coppo was a shield-bearer in the Florentine army at the epic battle of Montaperti in 1260, and was taken prisoner by the Sienese victors.

It is through their works that Bonaventura and Giunta, Coppo and Guido really emerge. Collectively, their known paintings—exclusive of those that may have been lost, ruined or destroyed—number fewer than a dozen. Yet these, added to other known products of their workshops, establish the presence of a new impulse in Italian painting, the evidence of inventive hands and fresh eyes at work.

Much of the impulse was owed to the deeds and preachings of St. Francis, and most directly in the case of Bonaventura and Giunta. The beloved *poverello,* the poor little man of Assisi, was still alive when they were youths. He is the subject of the sole surviving panel painting by Bonaventura. Of Giunta's four known works—all crucifixes—two were painted for Franciscan churches. One, later irreparably damaged in a fall, was painted at the request of the saint's intimate companion, Brother Elias, for hanging in the great basilica of St. Francis in Assisi.

In 1235, less than a decade after Francis died and was canonized, Bonaventura painted what is believed to be the first altarpiece in his honor *(pages 24-25).* The central figure is thoroughly traditional. It is Romanesque in its disproportion between tiny head and elongated body, Byzantine in its frontal pose and schematized face, and medieval in its depiction of Francis not as a man—as Giotto was to paint him in a more secular-minded day—but as an incarnation of the divine in man.

However, a new vibrancy enlivens the six small episodes flanking the central figure. Francis had preached brotherhood; Bonaventura's scenes, linking figures by glance and gesture, repeatedly stress the theme of contact between people. Francis had rejoiced in the physical world; Bonaventura's pictures abound in landscapes, buildings, objects. To be sure, he dealt with them in a way that later painters, skilled in optics and perspective, would find inept. He represented a mountain by jagged swells, merged the interiors and exteriors of buildings, tilted up tables so that the entire top was visible. But the wheel turns in art, and in the 20th Century Cézanne, Matisse and Picasso would again tilt up tables, proving anew, as Bonaventura did, that there is more than one road to visual reality.

Using an approach totally different from Bonaventura's, Giunta Pisano also reflected the humanism of Francis. In Giunta's crucifixes, Christ appears dead, in accord with Byzantine custom; the droop of the head, the stylized abdominal muscles, the red and white lines curving from Christ's side to symbolize blood and water, are all borrowed from Byzantine art. Nevertheless, Giunta's representation of Christ signaled a profound change. By accentuating the S-shaped curve of the body, so that it seemed to twist and strain, he produced an image of Christ not as a remote deity but as Francis saw Him: a Man whose agonies could be understood by all of suffering humanity.

Giunta vitally influenced subsequent depictions of Christ on the Cross. Many were mere imitations. But in Florence, Coppo di Marcovaldo added a dimension that makes his crucifix a landmark of painting. The face of Coppo's Christ *(pages 68-69)* is that of a Man from whose body the living animus has just departed. The eyes are empty sockets. The flesh around them seems shrunken. The curves of the mouth turn down in the manner of the tragic masks worn by actors in ancient Roman dramas. This effect was largely produced by what for Coppo's era was a remarkable technique: the use of shadows. With them he achieved so deep an anguish, so cosmic a despair that looking into the face of Coppo's Christ one almost feels the darkness that, according to St. Luke, descended during the Crucifixion "over all the earth."

Coppo's quiet revolution extended also to his depiction of the Madonna *(page 67)*. As he painted her, she is more maternal than regal. Her arm supports her Child; He turns to her and she to Him. To obtain this effect, Coppo employed a technique as rare for his time as the use of shadow: *contrapposto,* the positioning of the body so that one part turns in a different direction from another part. The result is a sense of action; Coppo's Madonna is far removed from the static Madonnas of Byzantium. She is also more corporeal, with obvious thighs and knees, substance, even bulk; she sits, not floats, on her throne. She looks out at the spectator with a novel directness of communication, and she wears an expression that is easily definable: a gentle sadness that bespeaks a prescience of her Son's fate. It is in Coppo's Madonna that one begins to discern the human emotions that were to become integral in Italian art.

The outpouring of fresh perceptions continued with Guido da Siena. His painting of the Madonna was close to Coppo's in using contrapposto and in portraying the figure full length and enthroned. But there was a hint of something new in the decorative grace and charm that pervaded Guido's work: the brocaded effect of the back of the throne, the gold piping of the Madonna's mantle, the delicate folds of her coif. By contrast Coppo's Madonna looked solemn and heavy.

Whether they knew it or not, Coppo, the Florentine, and Guido, the Sienese, were drawing the lines of an artistic rivalry that was to engage their cities for more than a century. This contest, in which no one lost and all art gained, began in earnest with two younger contemporaries of Coppo and Guido, two men destined to be giants of their time: Cimabue of Florence and Duccio of Siena.

Florence and Siena were old adversaries. Boundary disputes—although the two cities lay 40 miles apart—were one source of friction. Another irritant, to Florence, was Siena's wealth. Theoretically it should have been a poky little town; whereas Florence sat on a fertile plain along the Arno, with access to the sea, Siena was locked in by hills and watered only by two small streams that tended to go dry in the summer. But Siena had one annoying advantage. It ruled a stretch of the Via Francigena, a major trade route extending all the way from Rome to the Alpine passes. Commerce had made Siena a busy banking center—important enough, despite its persistent imperial sympathies in the continuing struggle between popes and emperors, to help handle the complex finances of the papacy.

Perhaps what irked Florence the most was the way the Sienese enjoyed themselves. Florentines, too, had their festivals and parades with banners and loud music, their gambling games, their gay flings. But in general they were hardheaded, down-to-earth, driven by overweening ambition. The Sienese, bankers notwithstanding, seemed better able to relax. They had a frank taste for the sensuous: for bright colors, rich fabrics, elegant décor. Their gilded youth rollicked in a unique club— *La Brigata Spendereccia,* the Spendthrifts' Brigade—whose avowed aim was to splurge in the pursuit of pleasure.

Moreover, the Florentines, while proud of their orthodoxy in religious matters, retained a strong streak of irony. The Sienese were intensely superstitious, and also believed implicitly in miracles. They had good reason for this belief on an occasion which proved to be a turning point of their affairs. Florence had drubbed another old foe, its seaward neighbor Pisa, and thus gained control of Tuscany's one good port. In the spring of 1260 it decided to spread inland as well, and sent a large army to polish off Siena. The desperate Sienese promptly mobilized—to appeal for aid from the Virgin. In a vast concourse they marched to the cathedral, praying, as one chronicler relates, "Mary Virgin, succor us . . . deliver us out of the claws of these lions. . . ." Two days later, although heavily outnumbered, they overwhelmed their attackers at Montaperti, capturing them by the thousands, Coppo di Marcovaldo included. Naturally, the surprised victors credited the outcome to the Virgin's intercession, and so they dedicated themselves and their city to her.

The victory was sweet but short. Florence, a faithful adherent of the papal cause ever since the days of Countess Matilda, looked to Rome for support against the pro-imperial Sienese. Less than three months after Montaperti the Pope placed Siena under an interdict, cutting it off from all ecclesiastical functions and privileges. He next threatened it with a crusade against its alleged heresies. Sienese business quickly dropped off; many firms were ruined. The papacy's intervention cost the Holy See dear; one banking house went bankrupt with the staggering loss of 80,000 florins in papal funds.

Siena drifted helplessly into the Florentine orbit. Its life went on at a muted pitch, nostalgic, even dreamy. Isolated and stripped of much of their territory and trade, the Sienese turned increasingly to religion and to art. By 1285 their leading painter, Duccio di Buoninsegna, had won enough fame to receive the unusual accolade of a commission from the former enemy camp, Florence, now in full sway over Tuscany.

Duccio was asked to paint a Madonna for the splendid new Dominican church of Santa Maria Novella. Known as the *Rucellai Madonna (page 54)* because it once adorned a chapel donated by a family of that name, it now hangs in the Uffizi Gallery of Florence. In the same room is a Madonna by Cimabue, called the *Trinita Madonna (page 73)* from its original location in the church of Santa Trinita. The two works insistently demand comparison. The one illustrates the spirit of Siena, the other the spirit of Florence. They are a tale, in paint, of two cities.

Their differences are all the more intriguing because in many ways they are very much alike. Both are huge works: Duccio's is nearly 15 feet high, Cimabue's nearly 13—almost twice the size of the Madonnas of Coppo and Guido. The new grandeur of Florentine church-building was not enough to explain this doubling of dimension. In any art form, increase of size reflects a more robust spirit, a psychological assurance, a coming of age. Jackson Pollock's enormous canvases, bursting upon the New York scene in the 1950s, created no greater excitement than did the works of Duccio and Cimabue in Florence in the 1280s.

Beyond their bigness, the two Madonnas share facial features reminiscent of the Byzantine: long noses, small mouths, almond eyes. In each case the Madonna is flanked by angels who touch her throne, lending a sense of tactile reality. Each artist shows awareness of a problem that was to loom ever larger in Italian painting: how to create an impression of depth. Duccio sets his throne at an angle; Cimabue draws converging lines on the Madonna's footstool, making it seem to recede in space. In general, except for the scriptural figures below Cimabue's throne, the two works are almost identical in format.

Yet there are dissimilarities—seemingly minor to today's casual beholder, but of urgent interest in the time of Duccio and Cimabue. Cimabue's throne is a massive piece of architecture; Duccio's is an exquisitely ornate seat. Cimabue's angels stand formally arrayed; Duccio's kneel in graceful obeisance to the Madonna. Cimabue's Christ Child sits grave and dignified; Duccio's Christ Child, thrusting His legs out, seems a playful, squirming infant. Cimabue's Madonna is plain, severe, female rather than feminine, a woman of large and unadorned mold; she was to be the precursor of the heroic women of Giotto, Masaccio and Michelangelo. Duccio's Madonna is softer, gentler, less solid; the fluid grace of her body is suggested by a sinuous gold line that edges her garment, descending in deep curves from her throat to her feet.

The *Trinita Madonna* is the work of a man whose aim is to make a statement, bluntly, almost fiercely, without attention to niceties of detail. The *Rucellai Madonna* is the work of a man wholly absorbed by sheer sensuous loveliness. More than most artists in history, Cimabue and Duccio mirrored the places that produced them, and helped shape the art of their cities accordingly. Florentine painting, like Florence itself, would be forthright, vigorous, dominant; Sienese painting would be less serious, more subtle, more charming. The divergent routes they took were well summed up by the critic Eric Newton. "In the struggle between truth and beauty which underlies all art," he wrote, "beauty is inclined to get the upper hand in Siena, truth in Florence."

In his private life and personality, Duccio seems to have been the prototype of the artist as nonconformer. He was rambunctious, willful, and prone to regard himself as above the law. From 1278 on his name appears frequently in Sienese municipal records, and not for the best of reasons. He refused to pay allegiance to the local representative of the Holy Roman Emperor. He failed to appear for military service. He was fined repeatedly, for disorderly conduct, for supposed sorcery, for nonpayment of bills. He must have lived well, even profligately, for although he commanded higher fees than other painters, he apparently put nothing by. After his death in 1319 his wife and seven children rejected his legacy—because it consisted entirely of debts.

Duccio was a handful for Siena, but also its pride and joy. Commissions of all sorts came his way. For the city itself, his activities were prolific and varied. He painted a dozen small chests built to hold official documents. For a number of years he decorated the wooden covers of the annual treasury report. He painted an altarpiece, since lost, for a chapel in the Palazzo Pubblico, the city hall. He served on a committee to choose the site of a civic fountain.

It is also likely that he profited from a slowly rising trend in private patronage. Individual donors had begun to fancy the idea of seeing themselves depicted in the presence of sacred personages. So, in a small panel painting, *The Madonna of the Three Franciscans,* Duccio portrayed the Virgin with a trio of monks (presumably the donors) kneeling at her feet, in the protective shelter of her skirt. For all the novelty of the treatment, Duccio retained a sense of proportionate values. By comparison with the Madonna, the monks are diminutive; one barely reaches to her ankles.

Sometime during the course of his busy career Duccio made a contact of lasting import to his own work and to all of Sienese art. The sculptor and architect in charge of constructing the cathedral façade was Giovanni Pisano. As his name indicates, he was a native of Pisa. He was also one of those phenomena in the development of art, a conscious link between old and new styles. The new style that he was instrumental in introducing into Italy was the Gothic, then in full flower in its homeland, France.

How a style travels from one country to another is easily determined in an age of jet planes and instant communication. Its routes at a time like Duccio's and Giovanni's can only be conjectured. Giovanni's father, Nicola, an equally gifted sculptor and architect, had worked at the Sicilian court of the Emperor Frederick II, alongside imported French artists. More recently, the French house of Anjou had taken over the Kingdom of Naples and Sicily, and was employing its own craftsmen. Members of a French monastic order, the Cistercians, had built abbeys around Rome and in Tuscany, bringing along the illuminated manuscripts, the carved ivories, and the architectural ideas of the Gothic. Possibly Giovanni Pisano, whose services were in much demand, journeyed north over the Alps and sketched the wondrous cathedrals of Paris and Chartres and Amiens. However they acquired their ideas of the Gothic, the Pisani embraced them, most notably in two great marble pulpits— one sculpted by Nicola for the Cathedral of Siena, the second by Giovanni for the Cathedral of Pistoia *(pages 48-51).*

Gothic elegance of line, harmony of form, and emphasis on beauty struck a particularly responsive chord in the Sienese. There was another fact, too, that they found irresistible. Gothic France shared, indeed exceeded, their adoration of the Virgin as the gentlest of divinities, who could sway her Son and allay the rigors of His justice. The French named armies after her, built their code of chivalry around her, and even revamped the game of chess—brought home from the East by crusaders—so that the queen, so called in the Virgin's honor, was the strongest piece on the board. The Gothic cathedrals themselves were

Don Matteo, a Cistercian monk serving as Siena's treasurer, is depicted on the cover of the city's financial records for 1339-1340 as he collects taxes from a citizen. Monks were usually appointed to watch the city coffers on the theory that they would be more honest than ordinary townsmen. Their ledgers were scrupulously detailed; they even listed such items as wages paid to soothsayers to predict the future of the republic, and the cost of a new copy of a book of laws to replace one torn up by the mayor's pet monkey.

paeans to the Virgin, hymns to her in stone, sculpture and glass. They were, in effect, her palaces, in which she reigned supreme.

Duccio's masterpiece embodied this Gothic ideal. Its very title—the *Maestà (pages 76-79)*, the Madonna in Majesty—was revealing; the avowed intent was to depict the Madonna in all the panoply of royalty, surrounded by her court of angels, apostles and saints. The scope of the work was unprecedented. Below the central panel was a predella, or base, containing seven scenes from the early life of Christ. Above the Madonna were seven pinnacled panels—a Gothic shape—devoted to scenes from the last days of the Virgin. Nor was this all. The entire back of the painting was covered with some 40 scenes from the life of Christ, from His ministry and miracles to His appearance before the apostles after the Resurrection.

Never had a painter set himself so infinitely detailed a task, and Duccio proved equal to it. Although most of the scenes are less than twice the size of this page, many include a dozen or more figures; moreover, the setting changes with each change of locale. Yet the scenes are superbly composed and often highly dramatic; Duccio's people express the whole range of human feeling, tenderness and awe, shame and incredulity, grief and exaltation. He experiments with composition, using architectural interiors to enclose his figures. And over all, the work has vividly beautiful coloring and grace of line. It is, as Duccio and the Sienese wanted it to be, a feast for the eye.

In a later century the *Maestà* was dismembered. The front and back were sawed apart. Some panels were lost, others were dispersed. Happily, the Sienese had no inkling of this outcome when, after three years, Duccio completed his labors. One day in June 1311 the *Maestà* was borne from his workshop to its place on the high altar of the cathedral. Shops were shut, a public holiday was proclaimed, alms were distributed to the poor, and a grand procession was organized, complete with trumpeters, drummers and bagpipers. "One by one," wrote a chronicler, "all the most worthy persons approached the picture with lighted candles in their hands and behind them came the women and children in devout attitudes. And they accompanied the said picture to the cathedral . . . while the bells sounded the Gloria, in homage to so noble a painting as this is."

Cimabue, too, produced a great masterwork, totally different from Duccio's in concept, style and impact: a vast fresco of the Crucifixion, painted on a wall of the left transept of the Upper Church of St. Francis in Assisi. Time has been as unkind to this work as human hands to the *Maestà*. Large patches of the fresco have crumbled, leaving bleak scars; because of chemical changes induced by the artist's use of white lead, many faces have turned black, conjuring up the appearance of a photographic negative. The *Crucifixion (pages 70-71)* is a ruin, but a magnificent ruin.

Cimabue's real name was Cenni di Pepo; the name by which he is better known is the Italian for "oxhead." It is a term that inescapably suggests brute strength and boundless energy. He was, according to one description, "so arrogant and haughty . . . that if anyone pointed out a fault or defect in his work, or if he discovered any himself . . . he immediately destroyed that work, however important it might be." In the *Crucifixion,* this quality of vehemence, of fury, was channeled positively, and with extraordinary results.

In the center is a huge figure of Christ. Above Him are angels; below, the mass of witnesses present at Calvary. To His left side stand the deriders, the priests, scribes and elders; to His right stand the believers, including the Virgin and Mary Magdalen. Christ's body hangs from the Cross in the slump of death. "And behold," runs the account by St. Matthew, "the veil of the temple was rent in twain from the top to the bottom; and the earth did quake and the rocks rent." Cimabue does not follow the Scriptural narrative by showing the earthquake, or the darkness mentioned by St. Luke. Instead, with a brilliantly inventive stroke, he substitutes a raging wind that serves to stir up an atmosphere of intense emotion while also conveying a sense of utter chaos.

Christ's loincloth billows out. The angels whirl in a frenzy of despair. The Magdalen flings up her arms in a hysterical burst of anguish. The Virgin's grief is quiet. She presses a hand over her heart as if, by a tremendous effort of will, she is containing the flood of her sorrow. This sense of restraint, of dignity appropriate to the mother of Christ, is emphasized by the arrangement of her hair in neatly coiled braids. Christ's deriders stand quietly, too; they have achieved their aim. But Cimabue adds a note of drama. He shows some of them pulling thoughtfully at their beards, as if wondering, too late, whether they have committed an appalling blunder.

Without discord, Cimabue mingled the elements of the supernatural and the mortal to make of one painting both a cosmic tragedy and a human drama. Despite the greatness of the later creations of Renaissance masters, his *Crucifixion* may well be the most powerful single fresco in the history of Christian art.

In Florence, Cimabue towered over his rivals. Apparently he was offered as of right almost every one of the most prestigious and rewarding commissions: the one major exception was Duccio's *Rucellai Madonna.* Other cities vied for Cimabue's services. At Assisi, in addition to painting the *Crucifixion,* he was the master in charge of all the frescoes in the sanctuary end of the Upper Church. For the apse of Pisa's cathedral, he executed a mosaic of St. John the Evangelist. His output is said to have been prodigious. Scholars still argue over which works are his and which those of his helpers and would-be imitators.

For the last three decades of the 13th Century Cimabue reigned unchallenged in the world of Florentine art. Then fortune faded; just how is concisely told in a verse in Canto XI of Dante's *Purgatory.* Listing those he knew who in life had been guilty of the sin of pride, the poet wrote: "In painting Cimabue thought to hold the field/ Now Giotto is acclaimed by all/ So that he has obscured the former's fame."

Thus, in the closing years of his life, Cimabue found himself eclipsed. The pill must have been a particularly bitter one to take. For, the story has it, Cimabue himself discovered the young Giotto, and guided his first steps on the road to immortality.

The Art of Two Cities

On the west coast of Italy, just above the knee of the Italian "boot," lies the province of Tuscany, a region that fostered two of the most influential schools of Italian painting, the Florentine and the Sienese.

Both as cities and as artistic forces, Florence and Siena were a study in contrasts. Florence, situated on the main north-south trade route, was Tuscany's capital, a beehive of social, economic, political and artistic activity. From this bustling milieu emerged Coppo di Marcovaldo and the impetuous Cimabue, who was described as being so proud that he would destroy even a very good work if it was too severely criticized. Both artists painted with vigorous self-assurance, often on huge panels. They were equally dedicated to evoking man's emotional nature and to solving the problems of picturing figures with a concern for three-dimensionality and space. It was Cimabue, most scholars believe, who may have taught Giotto his craft and who, thus, launched him on his brilliant career.

Siena is only 40 miles from Florence, but, tucked away in a remote mountain district, it was isolated from its rival city's frenetic urban pace. Sienese artistry developed in a different direction, and Siena's outstanding early painters, Guido da Siena and Duccio di Buoninsegna, communicated the essence of that distinctive style in works that are imbued with their love of colorful detail, light, and rhythmic and expressive line.

Coppo di Marcovaldo sought to heighten the illusion of depth in this large panel of the Madonna: dark shadows and bright highlights give dimension to the forms of Mary and the Christ Child, and it is clear that the angels are behind the throne.

Coppo di Marcovaldo: *Madonna and Child,* c. 1265-1270

STA. MARIA DEI SERVI, ORVIETO

Several conventions served early artists in their depiction of Christ on the Cross: a drooping head and closed eyes indicated the fact of death; stylized streams of blood and water spouting from open wounds denoted His torment.

Here, the Florentine Coppo di Marcovaldo has blended these traditions with striking innovations. The schematized musculature of Christ's abdomen and ribs and the stiff drapery of the loincloth reflect Byzantine practices. But the empty eye sockets, the lines of agony frozen in the face, the shadow obscuring the shape of the chin—these are Coppo's own creations.

Furthermore, the artist has pictured a body that sags with tangible weight, seeming to push the lateral scenes off the panel. Indeed, this concern with physicality would lead other artists to eliminate the side scenes altogether.

Coppo di Marcovaldo: *Crucifix*, probably late 1250s

PALAZZO COMUNALE, SAN GIMIGNANO

UPPER CHURCH OF S. FRANCESCO, ASSISI

Time has been unkind to this fresco of the Crucifixion. The original white lead pigment has oxidized to black, other colors have faded or flaked off, and sections of the plaster are destroyed. The painting still stands, however, as a monument to the genius of the great Cimabue.

Cimabue communicates his vision of the Crucifixion with vibrant energy. Angels tear their hair and beat their breasts as Mary Magdalen *(left, center)* throws up her arms in uncontrollable anguish; in counterpoint, Christ's friends and disciples *(far left)* stand in mute, introspective sorrow. Among them, St. John the Evangelist holds the Virgin Mary's hand; at the foot of the Cross kneels St. Francis (a forgivable anachronism, since the fresco is in the basilica dedicated to him).

At right center, Longinus, the soldier who had thrust his lance into Christ's side, looks up in sudden realization of Christ's divinity; at the far right, the Pharisees stand bewildered.

Cimabue: *Crucifixion,* c. 1280-1285

Cimabue was born Cenni de Pepo; Cimabue is a nickname that means "oxheaded," presumably in reference to his unflagging self-esteem. His pride was justified; he painted more convincingly than any of his predecessors. The figures in the fresco below seem to occupy three-dimensional space; they have shape, weight, depth. All the faces express character—compare Cimabue's gentle St. Francis *(below, right)* with the

austere image by Bonaventura Berlinghieri on page 24.

Most important, Cimabue strove to paint things the way they really looked. In one of the largest paintings of its time *(right),* nearly 13 feet high and more than 7 feet wide, the artist makes the parallel lines at the base of the throne seem to recede toward a point far behind the throne—a giant step toward the mathematically precise "vanishing point" of the Renaissance.

LOWER CHURCH OF S. FRANCESCO, ASSISI

Cimabue: *Madonna and Child Enthroned with St. Francis,* c. 1280-1285

72

GALLERIA DEGLI UFFIZI, FLORENCE

Cimabue: *Trinita Madonna*, c. 1285-1290

PINACOTECA, SIENA

Guido da Siena: *Reliquary Shutters,* 1255-1260, detail at right

While artists in Florence were striving toward ever-greater realism and monumentality, their counterparts in Siena were concentrating on imaginative scenes full of color and narrative detail. The first artist to voice the freshness and vitality of the Sienese spirit was Guido da Siena, who painted these wooden shutters.

Guido was endowed with a rich, if somewhat grisly, imagination, which he employed here in depicting the trials of four saints. In the top right panel he shows St. Bartholomew being flayed to death by pagans for spreading the Gospel. At lower right is the martyrdom of St. Catherine of Alexandria, being tortured on a spiked wheel for defeating 50 non-Christian philosophers in debate. At lower left, St. Clare repels lustful Saracens and saves Assisi with her prayers; in the detail from this scene, enlarged on the opposite page, she is seen praying in the monastery window while the unsuccessful invaders tumble from the roof.

At top left is St. Francis receiving the stigmata, the marks that symbolized Christ's wounds. Perhaps to authenticate the story that the event took place in the mountains, Guido included some roly-poly bears.

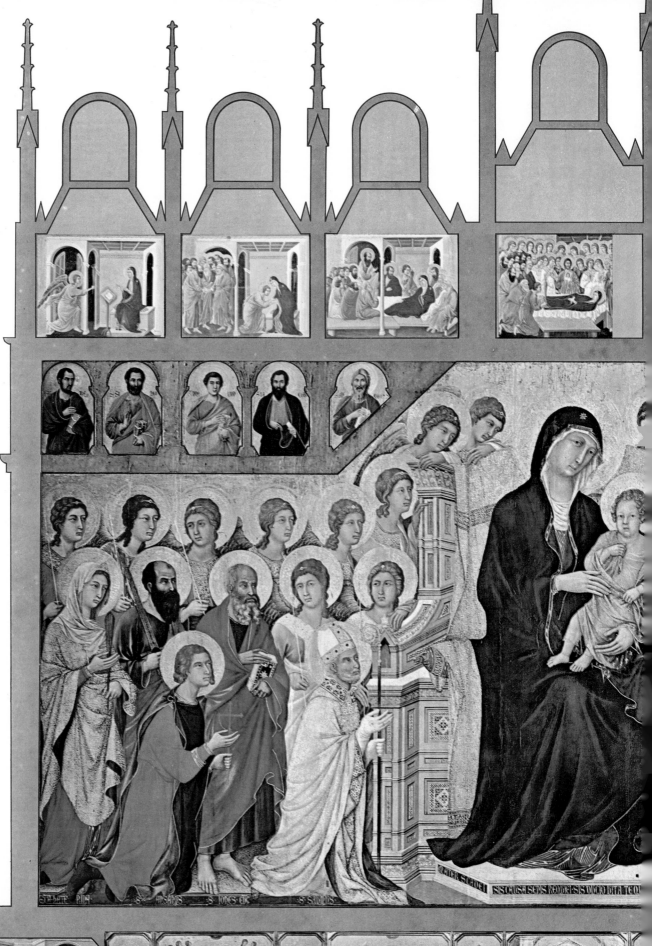

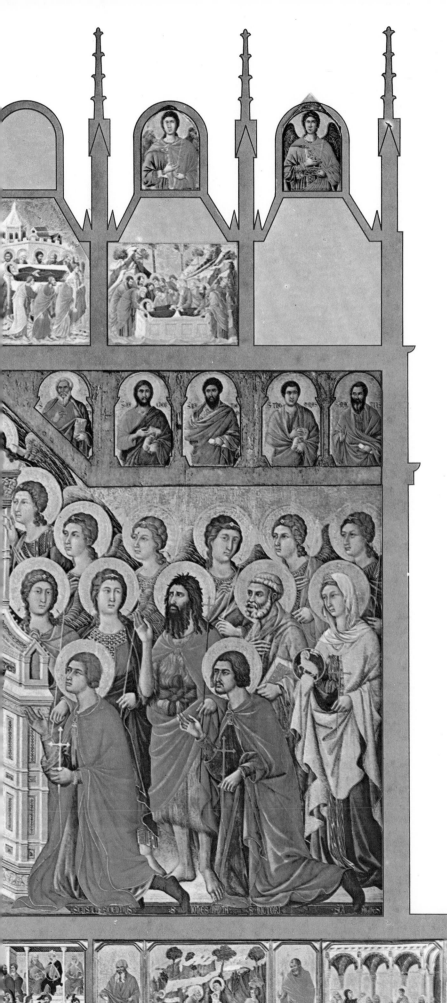

"*Mater Sancta Dei,*" reads the inscription on this huge panel painting, "grant peace to Siena, grant life to Duccio because he painted thee thus."

In 1308 Duccio was commissioned by the officials of the Siena Cathedral to paint a Madonna in Majesty, or *Maestà,* surrounded by prophets, apostles and angels, and episodes from the lives of the Virgin and Christ. After 32 months of devoted labor, he finished the painting, an altarpiece some 13 feet high and 14 feet wide and consisting of more than 40 individual panels on its front and back. His fee of 3,000 gold crowns was the highest ever paid for a work of this kind. The result, moreover, was a triumph for Duccio and for Siena. A contemporary chronicler wrote: "On the day when the *Maestà* was brought to the Duomo all shops were closed and the Bishop ordained that there should be a great procession. . . . All the townsfolk flocked together to see the *Maestà.* . . . The bells rang out a festive peal to welcome in this most noble altarpiece."

Since its unveiling, the *Maestà* has suffered. In the 18th Century, the front and back panels were separated and scattered; some were sawed up or marred, others were added to. Shown at left is a unique reconstruction of the *Maestà,* made under the direction of Dr. James H. Stubblebine from photographs especially taken for this project. The decorative framework that supported the panels has disappeared, but Dr. Stubblebine has provided a hypothetical framework (indicated in dark gray) and the order in which the panels probably appeared. Light gray areas indicate missing panels or missing portions of existing paintings.

An identifying key appears on page 193.

MUSEO DELL'OPERA DEL DUOMO, SIENA

The Sienese style reached a high point with Duccio, as these panels from the back of the *Maestà* show.

The scene at left is filled with story-telling details: so great is the jubilation of the townspeople at Christ's arrival that they throw down garments to provide a soft path; boys gather tree fronds to strew; everyone hurries to greet the Savior as He is escorted to the main gate of the town by His disciples, whose halos lend pictorial emphasis to His presence. The rhythm of Duccio's linear style and his brilliant colors add to the joy of the scene.

The gaiety of Christ's arrival is in sharp contrast to the majesty of His Crucifixion *(right)*. Silhouetted against a golden sky stand three stark crosses, a radical departure from the traditional solitary Cross. At the base of Christ's Cross the stony ground is stained with His blood. Mary, in a blue mantle, sways with emotion, and both the disciples on the left and the Pharisees on the right stand in awe.

Duccio: *Maestà;* "Entry into Jerusalem"

MUSEO DELL' OPERA DEL DUOMO, SIENA

Duccio: *Maestà;* "Crucifixion"

79

IV

A Boy from
the Hills

Frescoes by many important artists
decorate the basilica dedicated to St.
Francis in his birthplace, Assisi. Built
on the side of Mount Subasio, the
structure consists of two churches, one
built atop the other; the entrance to the
upper church is through the arched
doorway near the pyramid of steps at
the right; the lower church portal
faces an arcaded courtyard *(center)*.
Down the hill to the left, a huge
monastery adjoins the building.

The valley of the Mugello, where Giotto was born, lies about 20 miles north of Florence. It is a broad valley, ringed by high hills yet unoppressed by them; the guidebooks often recommend it as one of the mountainous areas of Italy where a walking tour is both possible and pleasant. On such a tour in the 19th Century, Giotto's passionate admirer, John Ruskin, explored the scenes of his idol's childhood. "Here and there," he wrote, "are seen the scattered houses of a farm grouped gracefully upon the hillsides; here and there a fragment of tower upon a distant rock; but neither gardens, nor flowers, nor glittering palace walls, only a gray extent of mountain ground, tufted irregularly with ilex and olive."

Ruskin thought it a "lonely" landscape, and even today the Mugello retains a quietude that seems resistant to time and change. An occasional electric pole obtrudes, and modern road-builders have circled the valley with highways that permit a quick glimpse of it by car as well as a leisurely look on foot. But the song of the lark and the voices of farmers still successfully compete with the sounds of the 20th Century.

In a house on one of the hillsides that captivated Ruskin's eye Giotto was born around 1267. There is no proof of the date; the supposition is based on a Florentine chronicle stating that Giotto—who is known to have died in 1337—lived to the age of 70. But the chronicler, Antonio Pucci, a poet who doubled as town crier, composed his account in couplets, and the suspicion lurks that he may have tailored the figure to fit; disposing of Giotto at 69 or 71 would have wrecked his rhyme. If scholars remain leery of this possible poetic license, Giotto's countrymen settled the matter to their own satisfaction by choosing 1967 as the year in which to celebrate his 700th anniversary.

Another controversy has attended the question of precisely where in the Mugello Giotto was born. Tradition named Vespignano, still only a hamlet with a handful of houses. Attached to one of these is a venerable, truncated tower with a marble plaque inscribed "Here Giotto was born" installed in 1850 by the widow who owned it. But since then, several Giotto enthusiasts have searched the local records and unearthed the fact that the tower had served in medieval times as a district administrative office. The discovery strengthened an alternate theory that Giotto may have been born at a hilltop farm about a mile away, at a site called Colle di Romagnano.

Local officials have met this turn of events with typical Tuscan aplomb. They decided that records notwithstanding, the Vespignano tower was more charmingly photogenic as an "official" birthplace. Purchased with civic funds, cleared of its rubbish and renovated as a Giotto museum, it is expected to draw many more pilgrims than the half-dozen or so a year who troubled to make the trek in past decades.

Giotto—that was his first name, and it may have been short for Ambrogiotto—was the son of a farmer named Bondone. Bondone was designated in a document by the Latin phrase *vir praeclarus,* an excellent man; presumably this meant that he was several cuts above the ordinary tiller of the soil. But this family distinction did not exempt Giotto from a country boy's customary chores, and it was while pursuing these labors at a tender age that he encountered the leading painter of the day, Cimabue, and made his fateful entry into the world of art.

So, anyway, goes the best-loved story in the Giotto legend. The most flamboyant teller of this tale was Giorgio Vasari, the tireless 16th Century biographer of some 150 artists, both his contemporaries and those of the past. Vasari's studies tend to be panegyrics; even for doubters, however, they make sprightly reading, and his version of little Giotto's meeting with his illustrious mentor-to-be, told as if at first hand rather than from a distance of almost 300 years, deserves quoting.

"When the boy had attained the age of 10 years," Vasari wrote, "he exhibited, in all his childish ways, an extraordinary quickness and readiness of mind. . . . Bondone then set him to watch a few sheep, and while he was following these from place to place to find pasture, he was always drawing something from Nature or representing the fancies which came into his head, on flat stones on the ground or on sand, so much was he attracted to the art of design by his natural inclination. Thus one day, when Cimabue was going on some business from Florence to Vespignano, he came upon Giotto, who, while his sheep were grazing, was drawing one of them from life with a roughly pointed piece of stone upon a smooth surface of rock . . . . Cimabue stopped in amazement and asked the boy if he would like to come and stay with him. Giotto replied he would go willingly if his father would consent. Accordingly Cimabue asked Bondone, who gladly consented, and allowed him to take his son with him to Florence."

Hollywood could not have hoped for a scene more neatly contrived. Indeed, Vasari's account might be dismissed as fictional except that Lorenzo Ghiberti told essentially the same story, more dryly, in his *Commentaries* only about 100 years after Giotto's death. Another writer, Leonardo da Vinci, referred in his *Codex Atlanticus* to the young Giotto's habit of sketching "goats and suchlike beasts" on rocks. There is, to be sure, a wholly different story which holds that Giotto and Cimabue did not meet until Giotto was adolescent and living in Florence. By this account, Bondone had moved his family to the city and obtained a job for Giotto with a wool merchant; instead of tending to his duties, the boy hung around artists' workshops until finally Cimabue took him in.

Although neither tale is provable, one fact emerges from both. Giotto found himself in Florence in his formative years, and at a time when the city itself was in a state of rampant growth. From the descriptions of him as a mature man, coarse-featured and ungainly, he could not have been much to look at even in the pink of youth. But he had natural talent, a bright mind, and eyes made keen by country vistas. There was no livelier place in Italy, at this period, to put them to use.

When Giotto began his apprenticeship, in 1280 or so, Florence had 45,000 people. The city had long since burst beyond the wall that marked its original limits, and was straining at the seams of a second wall. As in all cities in history, the poor and lowly made up the bulk of its inhabitants. Above them on the economic scale were craftsmen, shopkeepers and petty traders. At the top of the heap were the *magnati,* the magnates, the big-money men in banking and foreign commerce. Although small in numbers, this class was always open to a shrewd and ambitious man, whether he was a noble tired of a life of genteel poverty on his feudal lands or a commoner pushing up from the crowd.

Both economically and politically, the Florentines, disinclined by nature to bend to anyone's yoke, operated in an atmosphere exuberantly free of outside restraints. For one thing, they were no longer subject to the overlordship of the Holy Roman Emperor. The Empire had effectively ceased to exist in Italy with the death of the great Frederick II of the Hohenstaufen dynasty in 1250. Conrad IV succeeded his father, and for four years he tried to assert imperial power, but when he died in 1254, it was the signal for two decades of struggle for the imperial crown between Hohenstaufens and claimants backed by the papacy.

To prevent the resurgence of the "brood of vipers," as the Church had dubbed the Hohenstaufens, the papacy offered part of the imperial holdings in Italy to Louis IX of France, a monarch both devout and reliable. The King's younger brother, Count Charles of Anjou, swept into Italy with his army to establish his Angevin dynasty in Naples and Sicily. But there was still life in the Hohenstaufen brood. In the summer of 1267, Frederick II's 16-year-old grandson, Conradin, set forth to recapture his family's domains in Italy. Conradin, blond and handsome, advanced southward at the head of his army until, in August of the following year, he was defeated by the Angevins. The young Prince escaped but was captured soon after and beheaded, like a common felon, in the market square of Naples. With him ended the Hohenstaufen dynasty, but not the Pope's difficulties with secular rulers. For Charles of Anjou now began to oppose papal ambitions with an obstinacy reminiscent of Hohenstaufen days. Again the Pope looked for a counter-weight, and in 1273 succeeded in getting the German electors of the Holy Roman Emperor to select Rudolph of Habsburg. The Habsburgs were to occupy the imperial throne for centuries, but they rarely strayed out of their native Germany, and seldom interfered in Italian affairs.

Thus Tuscany came under Angevin control. Nevertheless Charles soon made it plain that Florence could pretty much run its own show. Florence fell to with its usual vigor. The new link with France provided

PALAZZO DEI CONSERVATORI, ROME

Arnolfo di Cambio carved this statue of his patron Charles of Anjou. A brother of King Louis of France, Charles claimed the Kingdom of Naples in 1266 at the Pope's invitation and by force of arms ended German domination in Italy. His French troops strengthened the political authority of the papacy.

special trading privileges in that country. Traditional Florentine support for the papal cause against the emperors also paid off. More and more, the papacy began to rely on the city's bankers to handle its finances. The fees were fat and fringe benefits plentiful. It was while collecting papal tithes in England that Florentine agents made the contacts with sheep raisers that led to the rise of the city's foremost industry, the weaving of woolen cloth.

Florence addressed itself with equal gusto to problems of internal politics, notably to the settlement of scores between two rival factions known as the Guelfs and the Ghibellines, whose tumultuous clashes had torn the city for years. The names as well as the rivalry were German in origin, stemming from an old feud over the imperial crown between the families of the Welfs and the Hohenstaufens. The latter's war cry, after a castle they owned, was "Waiblingen!" In Italy, partisans of the Hohenstaufen emperors came to be called Ghibellines, the papal adherents Guelfs. Gradually Ghibelline began to be equated with diehard feudal aristocrat, Guelf with rich commoner.

The implacable enmity between the foes appeared even in minute particulars. Whether a man cut his fruit across or down, or drank from a plain or chased goblet, or wore the feather in his hat on the right or left side, gave sign of his loyalties. Such trivia were taken very seriously. At dinner with a local noble, some visiting strangers made the tactical error of slicing their garlic in a way that revealed them as members of the enemy camp. Their host had them put to death.

In Florence, the warfare of local Guelfs and Ghibellines took on a ferocity unmatched elsewhere. Opponents were murdered in hot blood or cold calculation. In major upheavals, leaders of the losing faction would deem it wise to leave town, if indeed they were not driven from it. The victors would seize their fortunes and raze their properties; one of the great squares of present-day Florence, the Piazza della Signoria, emerged from a leveling of the houses of some luckless Ghibellines.

The decline of the imperial presence in Italy caused a corresponding shift in the power structure of Florence. The Guelfs were out—but not down—when Charles of Anjou arrived in Italy, and in him they scented salvation for their cause. Psychologically, the arrogant, hawk-nosed Charles may well have been more attuned to the lordly Ghibellines. Still, any foes of the Hohenstaufens were friends of his, and his string of military successes sent the Guelfs back to Florence in triumph.

By the time Giotto appeared on the scene the city was incontestably Guelf. This denoted far more than an end to strife. It signaled the rout of old-guard, stand-pat conservatism, and a victory for aggressive enterprise. The merchant oligarchs now in the saddle had no more love for the lower orders than the feudal rulers of yore. But the zeal with which they wooed profits brought unequaled prosperity to Florence—and a future of large opportunity for the country boy from the Mugello.

In 1282 an uprising against Charles of Anjou's iron rule in Sicily stripped him of half his kingdom, and his prestige plummeted. Coincidentally, that same year Florence set up its own government, a so-called priorate composed of six men chosen by the merchant guilds.

Always vigilant, the Florentines limited the priors to two-month terms and compelled them to live together in a rented house while they held office—the better to shield them from irate critics.

This curious system seems to have worked very well. With some added concessions of authority to the lesser craft guilds, plus some ordinances intended to provide a modicum of justice for the proletariat, it was to remain the basic format of the Florentine Republic for 200 years. A certain stability began to mark civic affairs, although never enough to make life dull. By the mid-1290s, the ruling Guelfs themselves had split into two factions—called the Blacks and the Whites—and a new era of bloodletting erupted on the streets of Florence.

Growing to manhood in the city, Giotto observed the ceaseless spectacle of human nature in the raw, and so did a sensitive, scholarly, well-born Florentine several years his senior: Dante Alighieri. Dante was destined to serve as a prior and later to be banished forever from his hometown as a White. In the course of his wanderings he would pour all of his revulsion against frail humanity—and his hopes for it—into a magnificent epic poem, the first to be written in Italian. Subsequent admirers would call his work the *Divine Comedy;* he named it simply the *Comedy.* In a masterly swipe at his compatriots, Dante noted on the title page that he was "A Florentine by Birth But Not in Character."

Of sturdier make than Dante, Giotto viewed the Florentine scene as a pragmatist, levelheaded, sardonic and frankly materialistic: in time he would profit heavily by hiring out looms to indigent weavers at steep charges. An earthy man without pretenses, he would tolerate the foibles of others, accept humanity as it was—and paint it accordingly.

O nly one anecdote survives of Giotto's apprentice days, but it suffices to reveal the man in the boy. As Vasari tells it, he was a relentless prankster. One time in the workshop, Cimabue was painting a face when he turned away from his work for a spell. Giotto seized the opportunity to paint a fly on the nose. When Cimabue resumed his labors, he tried to brush the fly off several times before he got the joke.

Apart from its disclosure of the precocity of Giotto's talent, the story is interesting for its insight into his self-assurance. Neither then nor later would he kowtow to anyone; popes and princes, no less than ordinary people, would provide targets for his wit and candor. If Cimabue expected deference from his young charge, he was to be disappointed. A capacity for awe was absent from Giotto's make-up.

Vasari fails to report whether Cimabue lost his temper over the incident of the fly, but apparently no permanent ill will resulted. Although positive evidence is lacking, it is believed that Cimabue included Giotto among the assistants who accompanied him on trips away from Florence to fulfill the commissions with which he was besieged. From the standpoint of Giotto's subsequent development, the most important stop on the itinerary of these conjectured early trips was Rome. While artists elsewhere were painting on wood, Roman artists were still nurturing the ancient tradition of fresco, and Giotto may have learned from them the fundamentals of the technique that he was to bring to brilliant fruition.

Equally crucial to Giotto's future in art was the presence in the papal

SANTA MARIA NOVELLA, FLORENCE

This praying figure, a detail from a mural by Andrea Orcagna in Florence, is believed to be Dante Alighieri, author of the *Divine Comedy.* One of the great classics of literature, the poem describes Dante's journey through Hell, Purgatory and Heaven, at times guided by the Classical poet Virgil, at others by the author's beloved Beatrice. Dante's writings established his native Tuscan dialect as the principal literary language of Italy, replacing Latin.

capital of two men who were becoming acknowledged giants of painting and sculpture. The painter Pietro Cavallini was a native Roman. The sculptor Arnolfo di Cambio was a Tuscan who had ventured afield to win his renown—and the patronage of Charles of Anjou. Scholars argue intensively over many aspects of Giotto's career, but most of them agree that he was beholden both to Cavallini and to Arnolfo.

In this light, it is all the more noteworthy that both artists, despite their different media, had essentially the same aim: to give their figures a convincing sense of substance. In painting, the concept of three-dimensionality was still relatively untried; yet Cavallini dealt skillfully with it, deriving his ideas from Classical statuary. A characteristic Cavallini figure had the naturalistic look as well as the draped toga of an ancient Roman memorialized in marble.

Arnolfo had followed the trail from Classical to Gothic, training under the celebrated sculptor Nicola Pisano and teaming up for a time with Nicola's son Giovanni. He had, however, evolved his own interpretation of the Gothic sculptural style that they had helped spread through Italy. The figures he carved were bulky rather than graceful, austere rather than endearing; when he grouped them, however, the effect was not crowded but spacious and harmonious. Giotto, although he worked in only two dimensions, would eventually achieve the same sculptural quality, the same union of the monumental and the simple, the same serenity of arrangement.

Whether or not he first saw Arnolfo's works in Rome, Giotto was able to scrutinize them on his own home ground sometime before the end of the century. More affluent than ever, exuding self-confidence, Florence was launched on a great wave of expanding, building and beautifying. In 1284 construction started on its third wall, some 40 feet high and five miles long. With this extension of its limits, it began to tear down modest structures of the past and replace them with splendid edifices. In construction contracts, one clause cropped up with increasing frequency. It adjured the men responsible for each new work to make it *più bella che si può*—as beautiful as possible.

In the decade and a half from the start of the third wall to the century's close, four familiar landmarks of present-day Florence began to change the skyline. The Dominicans at the western end of town and the Franciscans at the eastern end, fiercely competing for prestige, razed their respective churches of Santa Maria Novella and Santa Croce. The original small and simple buildings made way for great and lavish houses of worship whose elegance owed much to Gothic prototypes. In the center of Florence the foundations were laid for a bigger and better cathedral. Not far away, a massive structure was going up to house the priorate and to furnish Florence with a suitably impressive town hall, the Palazzo della Signoria. Fittingly, the building fronted on the square created by the destruction of Ghibelline homes.

The chief master of works at both the Cathedral and the Palazzo was Arnolfo—invited home, in the words of the contractual agreement, as "the most famous and expert master in the art of ecclesiastical building of any known in the region." Invested with the primary task of arch-

SANTA CECILIA IN TRASTEVERE, ROME

Pietro Cavallini was the dominant painter in Rome when Giotto worked there at the close of the 13th Century. His attachment to Classicism is seen in this detail from his *Last Judgment*, in which an apostle wearing a toga is seated like an ancient Roman senator. Giotto knew Cavallini's work and in his own later painting, particularly in the Arena Chapel frescoes *(pages 113 to 129)*, he strove for a similar sense of subdued grandeur and a dignified portrayal of the human figure.

tectural planning, he also carved figures and groups for the Cathedral façade. Three centuries later they were removed: a few remain in the Cathedral museum. In their time, they were a civic wonder—and a source of recurrent inspiration to Giotto.

Giotto himself took part, less prominently, in the city's dress-up campaign. His earliest attributed work there is a crucifix designed to be hung on a choir screen at the new Santa Maria Novella, his own parish church. It was painted sometime around 1290, several years after Duccio of Siena painted the *Rucellai Madonna* for the same interior.

The immense size of Giotto's crucifix—nearly 19 feet high—conforms to the custom of the day; yet there are subtle departures from other conventions. Christ's body is not tautly S-shaped, as Cimabue and Coppo and Giunta had depicted it, but composed in the calm dignity of death. On panels beyond the arms of Christ are half-length figures of the Virgin and St. John. Their faces are clearly, expressively sad, and they do not look out, but turn toward Christ. The crucifix shows no other figures, no small scenes, virtually no embellishment of any kind. It has a theme, pathos, and treats it sparingly. It is not just a painting on a panel, but a picturization of emotion.

One parishioner was so stirred by the work that he left money in his will for oil to keep the lamp perpetually aflame before it. Thus was Giotto's hold on the spectator foretold. A new and greater test of that strength awaited him at the most resplendent church in all of Italy, the shrine of the humble St. Francis at Assisi.

The Basilica of St. Francis *(page 80)* is a sight of unabashed grandeur, a vast citadel of pink limestone spread over more than an acre. It is not a single church but two, one superimposed on the other. The Lower Church has the heavy pillars and somber look that are typical of the Romanesque; the Upper Church has the stained-glass windows and lofty vaults that are typical of the Gothic.

Although architecturally dissimilar, the two interiors share one remarkable feature: almost every available inch of wall and ceiling is given over to frescoes, portraying hundreds of scenes and separate figures. The foundation of the Basilica was built in 1228; the final decorative flourishes were not applied until 1369. Over this protracted interval Assisi was the proving-ground for countless painters both major and minor, and an exchange place for stylistic ideas. The frescoes in the Basilica make it a unique repository of 13th and 14th Century Italian art, a treasure trove of inestimable value.

What Francis himself would have thought of all this magnificence presented in his name may be surmised. As he had indicated in his testament, he was strongly opposed to the idea of fixed abodes for the Franciscans. "Let the brothers take great care," he wrote, "not to receive churches, habitations, and all that men build for them." Some years later Francis' old comrade, Brother Giles, viewed the works at Assisi and made a bitter jest. "All you lack are wives," he told the monks who had shown him around. "After throwing Poverty overboard, it is easy enough to throw Chastity as well."

There were many Franciscans who, like Giles, recoiled at Assisi's splen-

SANTA MARIA NOVELLA, FLORENCE

In 1312, Ricuccio Pucci, a parishioner of Santa Maria Novella in Florence, made a will leaving funds for a perpetual lamp to burn before a crucifix "by the illustrious painter, Giotto," in his church. This is the only contemporary documentation of the Crucifix *(above)* and is important in the dispute over whether Giotto actually painted it. Some experts find the work old-fashioned and derivative; others feel it combines both Giotto's power and his emotional reticence—and cite Pucci's will as evidence.

dors. There were many others who argued that the order's acquisition of churches and convents did not contravene the preachings of Francis if the monks themselves owned nothing. The two factions—the Spirituals and the Conventuals—were to clash repeatedly, but no power could halt the momentum of the drive to turn Assisi into a showplace of propaganda and an object of pilgrimage.

The old controversies have long since been stilled; another has risen in their stead. It has none of the violence of the early disputes, but it has scarcely less fervor or partisanship. The weapons in this controversy are words, the protagonists are art scholars, and the bone of their contention is the question of what—if anything—Giotto painted at Assisi.

That this question even exists would come as a revelation to most Assisi visitors. Many go there primarily to see Giotto's work, and the Basilica's guides deal fleetingly, if at all, with the attacks on its authenticity. The traditional belief, unbroken for more than five centuries, has been that Giotto, sometime during the 1290s, painted one of Assisi's chief glories: the cycle of 28 frescoes of St. Francis that adorns the Upper Church. Unfolding in stately procession around the lower part of the walls of the nave and the entrance, the cycle presents a sequence of scenes from the saint's life; each fresco is about nine feet high and seven-and-a-half feet wide. In subject matter, the scenes *(pages 92-99)* reflect the changes that overtook the rapidly growing Franciscan order. They are based not on the simple, unaffected accounts of Francis by his own contemporaries, but on the imposing official biography that supplanted them, written by the strong-minded Bonaventura, minister-general of the Franciscans from 1257 to 1274.

These frescoes, like all others at Assisi, are unsigned. However, this is only one of the obstacles to identification. In 1809 Napoleon's invading troops looted and vandalized the Basilica, and in the confusion following this disaster someone lost, stole or destroyed the friary's account books for the years up to 1352—records that might have shown which artist was paid for what work. Thereafter, all that could sustain the tradition linking Giotto to Assisi were hearsay accounts of a few writers of his own time and the next centuries.

Then, in 1912, an eminent German scholar, Friedrich Rintelen, tossed a bombshell. Dismissing both tradition and the early written references, Rintelen produced a point-by-point comparison of the stylistic differences between the St. Francis cycle and Giotto's frescoes in the Arena Chapel at Padua—work known as his beyond doubt. Rintelen's shattering conclusion was that the same hand could not have done both, and that the painter of the St. Francis frescoes was an unknown master. Specifically, he found that the Assisi painter rendered landscape and architectural detail more precisely than Giotto, but lacked his ability to relate figures to their surroundings and to unify his compositions.

Rocked by Rintelen's study, scholars on both sides of the Atlantic began to align themselves. A furor of argument arose that the saint of brotherly love, who was the subject of the questioned frescoes, would have found distinctly painful. Generally, American scholars sided with Rintelen against the Italians. Barrages of academic epithets such as "doctrinaire prejudice" and "wishful thinking" were backed by microscopically detailed comparative studies of the Assisi and Padua frescoes down to the last angel, halo, rock and tree. One of the major arguments made by the pro-Giotto forces was that whereas in Padua Giotto was free to express his own conceptions, at Assisi he had to adhere strictly to the Bonaventura biography of Francis, in effect serving simply as an illustrator of a highly specific text.

In the half century since Rintelen, a number of subtheories have appeared. One holds that Giotto did not paint the St. Francis cycle, but did paint parts of another fresco cycle in the Upper Church, scenes from the Old Testament including two frescoes featuring the Biblical figure of Isaac. Advocates of this theory assert that Giotto is the unknown "Isaac Master" to whom these works *(page 91)* have been attributed. Another theory holds that Giotto painted some but not all of the St. Francis frescoes, perhaps the first 19; partisans of that theory have been cheered by a recent analysis of the "mural topography" of the frescoes by Professor Millard Meiss of the Institute for Advanced Study at Princeton and an Italian art restorer, Leonetto Tintori. Using magnifying lenses and powerful lighting, Meiss and Tintori examined overlapping patches of fresco and the patterns in which the wet plaster was laid down and concluded that the St. Francis cycle was painted by at least three masters with three distinctive styles.

The heart of the argument, however, remains as it emerged from Rintelen's study. Could the same artist have painted both the St. Francis and Padua frescoes? Could they, perhaps, have been respectively painted by the young Giotto and the mature Giotto? In asking these questions, the disputants also raised a larger question applicable in every era of art: can the essential substance of an artist's style change?

Professor Richard Offner, the leading American proponent of Rintelen's thesis, argued that it could not—that this substance "remains constant, as indeed in the common lives of men." Just as a man's glance, voice, gait and scent cannot vary, Offner declared, so an artist's style cannot fundamentally vary, and changes of style "are chiefly changes in degree of tension and not in their essential nature."

In retort, Professor Frank Jewett Mather, the leading American defender of the Giotto-at-Assisi theory, argued that artists were human beings rather than "mechanisms which produce problems to be solved by style critics." Point out to such a critic the dramatic style differences in the work of a Titian or Rembrandt or Velasquez, Mather asserted, and the critic can call to his defense only an "entirely mythical witness called 'The Medieval Artist.' . . . An odd fish; he keeps the straight line in which his master started him, never hesitates, never reconsiders, never experiments at large; in short, the medieval artist is pretty well immune to all influence except that which catapulted him on his career."

Barring the discovery of a document that settles the issue with absolute finality, the debate over Giotto and the St. Francis cycle continues to be a stand-off. But insofar as it demonstrates that the eye of the beholder—critic or amateur—remains the ultimate judge of a work of art, it is a debate that Giotto himself would assuredly have relished.

Mystery of Assisi

In 1228, only two years after the death of St. Francis, construction was begun on a huge basilica in his honor at Assisi. Many of the saint's followers regarded the magnificence of the project as a perversion of Francis' ideal of poverty, but, fortunately for art lovers, other minds prevailed. The basilica was decorated with frescoes and paintings by some of Italy's greatest masters, including Cimabue, Pietro Lorenzetti and Simone Martini.

For hundreds of years it was generally accepted that Giotto, too, had painted at Assisi, specifically the cycle of 28 frescoes depicting the life of St. Francis in the upper church. But in 1791, Guglielmo della Valle, a Franciscan father and an amateur art historian, noting certain stylistic discrepancies between the scenes, suggested that Giotto had not painted all of them. In the next 50 years other critics supported this view, adding the notion that Giotto painted nothing at Assisi; since then the controversy has flourished.

Unfortunately, no document exists to solve the mystery conclusively; for example, there are no ledgers or contract records to show that Giotto was assigned to the work or was paid for it. Those who believe that Giotto painted the St. Francis cycle cite tradition and commentaries by later writers. Doubters rely on a stylistic comparison with known Giotto works.

On the pages that follow, which show a number of the designated scenes from Assisi, are some of the arguments for and against attributing them to Giotto.

Three panels from the St. Francis cycle, depicting scenes from the saint's life, span a bay in the upper church at Assisi. The frescoes flanking the window are episodes from the life of the Biblical patriarch Isaac. Some scholars believe that Giotto painted the Isaac scenes; others attribute them to an unknown painter, the "Isaac Master."

St. Francis scenes *(left to right): Innocent III Approving the Order, The Miracle of the Chariot, The Vision of the Thrones*

St. Francis Giving His Cloak to a Poor Knight

In his youth, Francis, the son of a wealthy cloth merchant, was undecided whether to follow in his father's footsteps or to pursue the career of a knight. To try out the soldierly life he enlisted in the papal army and set off to do battle in southern Italy. Before leaving the environs of Assisi—recognizable in the background of the scene above *(left)*—Francis met a poorly dressed but noble knight and without hesitation stripped off his own costly cloak and gave it to the man, an act that foreshadowed his later life of charity and poverty.

Shortly after this generous deed, Francis was told in a vision to return to Assisi and to "repair My House, which is falling in ruins"—the first sign of his divine calling to aid the Church. To finance his mission, Francis took some goods from his father's stock; the old man, furious, had him temporarily imprisoned. In the dramatic scene at right

St. Francis Renouncing His Earthly Possessions

Francis is seen returning everything he had stolen to his father, and the clothes he was wearing, while the Bishop of Assisi shields the naked youth with a rough cloth. With this act Francis renounced his inheritance and accepted God as his true Father.

Argument: Those who doubt that Giotto painted the St. Francis cycle contend that the highly descriptive landscape and intricate architectural backgrounds in these scenes distract from the central action; they feel that Giotto, a supremely economical storyteller, would never have allowed so many elements to compete for the viewer's attention. Those who disagree with this view insist that the story's local setting and the fact that it had occurred so recently—within the century—would have led any artist to include recognizable details.

The Dream of Pope Innocent

Despite the arduous life of poverty, chastity and
obedience to God that Francis advocated, he quickly
attracted a band of devoted followers who, like himself,
preached the Gospel and lived as mendicants. In 1209, at
the age of 27, Francis went to Rome and sought to gain
approval for his new order from Pope Innocent III. In his
first interview, the Pope, suspecting that the young man
was just another overzealous reformer, indicated that he
would refuse him. But Francis prevailed upon him to
reconsider and was granted an audience for the
following day. That night in a dream the Pope saw
Rome's Lateran Basilica, the Mother of Churches, about
to topple when suddenly a man rushed up and supported
its weight with his shoulder *(above)*. The man was
Francis. The next day the Pope endorsed the new order.

Francis now began to preach throughout Italy. Passing

The Expulsion of the Demons from Arezzo

by Arezzo with Sylvester, a member of his brotherhood, he found a bloody battle raging. Demons had prodded the citizens into civil war and were dancing gleefully overhead, watching the slaughter. Francis sent Sylvester to the city gates *(above, right)* while he knelt in prayer. Miraculously, the demons were exorcised.

Argument: In the 1960s, an art historian, Professor Millard Meiss, and a master art restorer, Leonetto Tintori, completed an examination of all the Assisi frescoes. They found that the paint in some of the scenes, including the two shown above, contained white lead, the substance whose extensive use had caused such serious deterioration in the Cimabue fresco shown on pages 70 and 71. No known work of Giotto's shows any signs of having been painted with this material.

One of the many miracles associated with St. Francis occurred a fortnight before Christmas in the year 1223. The saint was traveling from Rome to Assisi when he stopped in the little town of Greccio, where he proposed to celebrate the Nativity, his favorite holy day. After saying Mass and preaching a sermon on the joys of heaven, Francis knelt before a little manger in the midst of townspeople and local priests. Just then, the figurine of the Christ Child, which Francis had requested, was seen to come alive and smile radiantly at the saint. This miraculous episode became one of the most popular stories about St. Francis and, although the legend describes the scene as taking place in the mountains, it is pictured here as occurring within the confines of a church.

On another occasion, Francis and two of his monks were traveling in the mountains on an exceedingly hot day with

The Miracle of the Spring

a peasant who had lent them a donkey. They walked all morning with nothing to drink; toward noon the peasant pleaded with Francis to find him water or he would die. Francis knelt and prayed *(above)*, whereupon a spring gushed from the rocks and the grateful peasant threw himself down to quench his thirst.

Argument: The 16th Century painter and biographer

Vasari, who credited the entire St. Francis cycle to Giotto in his *Lives of the Artists,* singled out the scene at the spring for particular praise. "One of the most beautiful of these [frescoes]," he wrote, "represents a thirsty man, whose desire for water is pictured in the most lively manner as he kneels on the ground to drink from a spring, with such wonderful reality that one might imagine him to be a real person." Doubters point to the unconvincing landscape.

Francis and his followers were once invited to share a
meal with the Knight of Celano, a man known for his
generosity to the poor. Before attending the meal, Francis
received divine forewarning that the knight was about to
be sent to heaven as a reward for his good deeds, and he
advised the devout man to confess, make arrangements for
his household and prepare himself. While the guests were
waiting to be seated, the knight suddenly and mysteriously

died *(above)*; miraculously, St. Francis' extraordinary
prediction had come true.

The greatest miracle of Francis' life occurred only a few
months before his own death. Having spent a lifetime
devoting himself to the suffering of others, the saint was
finally blessed with a precious sign of Christ's suffering: he
received the stigmata, wounds symbolic of the Crucifixion.
After Francis died, his body was brought to San Damiano,

The Lament of the Poor Clares

in Assisi, the home church of the Poor Clares, a sister order founded on the Franciscan example. It was there he had begun his service to the Church and there St. Clare herself wept over his body *(above)*.

Argument: The boy in the tree in the second episode closely resembles a figure that is known to be by Giotto (see scene 26 on page 121). Nevertheless, doubters insist that the composition of both scenes is very unlike Giotto's work. In the one at the left, for example, the important figure, the knight, is off-center and almost obscured by his mourners. Giotto, they maintain, always arranged the details of his compositions so that they instantly focused attention on the key event, the spiritual heart, of the scene.

For comparison, a set of frescoes indisputably painted by Giotto is pictured on pages 113 through 129.

V

The
Masterwork

In a land of savage animosities, Giotto remained singularly above the fray. So far as is known, he had no enemies and no detractors. A man of even temper and robust humor, he went his way unscathed by the clashes of his compatriots, increasingly sought after and successful.

The sole surviving clue to his views on the rancorous issues of his time is a long poem he wrote attacking poverty—an obvious thrust at those followers of St. Francis who clung to his precepts of self-denial. To commend poverty, Giotto wrote, was hypocritical; it was a condition that led to thievery, violence, corruption and the dishonor of women, and the society that condoned it was the weaker for it.

Giotto's argument had practical as well as philosophical implications. At one point in the furious struggle within the Franciscan order over the austerity issue, its proponents banned "curious and unnecessary ornaments" in Franciscan churches—a category in which they included "pictures, carvings, windows, columns and the like." Had this policy prevailed, some of Giotto's works would never have been done.

But the papacy, the ultimate arbiter of the Franciscan controversy, grew less and less tolerant of the pro-poverty faction, the so-called Spirituals. During the period of Giotto's emergence as an artist, most of the reigning popes supplied both moral and financial support for the splendors of Assisi. The ever-larger crowds of pilgrims thronging the basilica on the slopes of Mount Subasio gave ample proof that art helped rather than hindered the purposes of the Church.

As the 14th Century approached, the papacy began to look to the enhancement of its own capital. The city on the Tiber had lost its old imperial aura; the marble remnants of antique glories stood deep in weeds. Mud and refuse clogged the streets, and the dangers to life and limb were compounded by the incessant public brawling of local clans. In recent decades the popes had taken to absenting themselves with increasing frequency, preferring the more salutary air of country retreats.

Compared to the later great programs for decorating Rome in which Michelangelo and Raphael and Bernini took part, the plans of Pope Boniface VIII, who began his reign in 1294, were modest. They were

Kneeling humbly, the donor of the Arena Chapel in Padua, Enrico Scrovegni, presents a model of the building to the angel Gabriel, standing at center, and to Mary in two of her guises: as the Virgin of Charity (extending a hand), and as the Virgin of the Annunciation (accepting the gift). A monk supports the model. The scene is a detail from a fresco by Giotto in the chapel.

Detail from *The Last Judgment*

also fated to be short-lived. But they were a start, and they brought Giotto to Rome as one of the most illustrious practitioners of his art in all Italy. The city had its own reservoir of talented painters, stone-workers and mosaicists; Pietro Cavallini, Rome's best-known painter, was active. By now, however, Giotto was the artist whose cachet was beginning to be desired above all others.

History deals capriciously with documents, and while it has left no record of the exact dates of Giotto's Roman stay, it has preserved a piece of evidence that the sojourn was a lengthy one. The evidence is a legal paper written when Giotto was back home in Florence in 1313. Apparently he had been having his troubles with a balky ex-landlady in Rome, and he appointed a proxy in that city to recover a number of household effects, bedding included. From Giotto's listing of the domestic comforts with which he had surrounded himself when in Rome, biographers have deduced that he lived there for several years—long enough to have turned out a good deal more than the few works that survive.

Although time has obscured the full extent of Giotto's achievements in Rome, the accounts of early writers leave an impression of a virtuoso in the prime of his powers, moving confidently about the city on a variety of commissions: designing mosaics, illustrating a cardinal's manuscripts, painting in one church a Crucifixion and in another a series of medallions of the prophets, in a third church decorating the apse.

Ghiberti and Vasari between them credited Giotto with the lion's share of the redecoration of old St. Peter's. Built on the majestic lines of an imperial Roman basilica, this hallowed place of early Christianity had weathered almost 10 centuries by Giotto's time, and was to stand for nearly two more before being torn down to make way for the present St. Peter's. The combined testimony of Ghiberti and Vasari ascribe to Giotto the design of the mosaics of the huge nave of the ancient church, five frescoes of the life of Christ, another fresco series of scriptural scenes, and diverse panel paintings. These, Vasari indicated, were too numerous to mention. Some, he wrote in 1568, "have been restored by other artists in our own day, and some have been either destroyed or carried away from the old structure of St. Peter's during the building of the new walls."

Although nothing remains that definitively shows Giotto's hand, two works for the basilica that tradition has assigned to him have eluded the wreckers. By the same whim of preservation that kept intact the record of his joust with his Roman landlady, there survives a document naming the price he received for each of the two works. This document is a roster of benefactors of the Church and their gifts; included in the roll is Cardinal Jacopo Gaetani degli Stefaneschi, a nephew of Pope Boniface, canon of St. Peter's, and Giotto's devoted patron. For a mosaic depicting Christ's rescue of Peter from the Sea of Galilee, the Cardinal paid Giotto 2,200 gold florins; for an altarpiece, 800 gold florins. These sums were so munificent by prevailing standards that scholars suspect prideful padding on Stefaneschi's behalf. Even so, the figures offer a measure of Giotto's stature at the time.

The mosaic, known as the *Navicella,* or *The Little Boat*—was originally in the courtyard of old St. Peter's; it is now in the portico of the successor church, opposite the main door of the basilica. The altarpiece, a polyptych of six panels topped by Gothic gables, once adorned the basilica's high altar; it now hangs in the Vatican art gallery.

One other Roman work attributed to Giotto survives. It is a fragment of a fresco that shows Pope Boniface VIII, attended by two prelates, proclaiming the Jubilee of 1300. The strong characterization of the faces represents portraiture unusual for the time. The original, according to a drawing of it still extant, showed many more figures, including dignitaries of the papal court and a crowd of citizens on horse and on foot. Among the spectators was a king, and he was represented as just another member of Boniface's audience.

To contemporary viewers of the fresco, the studied placement of king in subordinate relation to pope must have had the urgent interest of a newspaper headline today. Boniface, one of the toughest autocrats ever to occupy the papacy, had renewed the drive for supremacy in matters temporal as well as spiritual. Having bested the Hohenstaufens and kept a rein on subsequent rulers of the Holy Roman Empire, the Church had now turned to dealing with a cocky new breed of secular monarch, the Kings of England and France. Boniface's attempts to bring them to heel were to end in utter failure, with results that would affect Italy for longer than Giotto's lifetime.

Giotto's *Navicella* (Little Boat), a mosaic showing Christ walking on the Sea of Galilee, was originally set above the entrance to the atrium opposite the main doorway of the old St. Peter's Church in Rome. Its placement is known from an engraving *(top)* made in 1673; the original design is believed to be revealed in an early 15th Century drawing. However, the mosaic has been moved and restored so often (it is now in the portico of the new church) that not one original tile may remain.

Boniface was not a man of endearing charm. That Giotto got along with him may have been due to the Pope's growing preoccupation with politics at the expense of art, or to the artist's equable nature and his solid standing with the hierarchy; he was, in effect, a court painter, wholly attuned to the wishes of the papal establishment. Unlike the stormy but warm relationship between Michelangelo and Pope Julius II in a later century, the rapport between Giotto and his august patron seems to have been based on a brisk awareness of mutual advantage.

In a host of other people Boniface inspired sheer loathing. Among them was Dante, whose permanent exile from Florence began after a futile mission to the Pope to dissuade him from meddling in the city's internal disputes; some of the most scorching words in the *Divine Comedy* were reserved for Boniface. Admirers of the previous Pontiff, the aged and ascetic Celestine V, who ruled for a few reluctant months and then abdicated, whispered that Boniface had induced the old man to quit; they claimed that he had counseled Celestine in the guise of a seraph, communicating with him one midnight by way of a speaking tube concealed under the papal pillows. This was rumor, but some of the proven facts were as unpalatable. Boniface was notoriously given to venting his spleen. He kicked one envoy in the face, and he threw ashes in the eyes of an archbishop who was kneeling to receive them on his head.

Edward I of England and Philip IV of France were hard to intimidate. The Pope's quarrel with them started over their decisions to help finance their nationalistic ambitions—and their campaigns against each other—by taxing the clergy in their realms. As Boniface saw it, Church revenues were taxable only by the Church. In 1296 he threatened to excommunicate any lay ruler who levied such a tax and any prelate

BIBLIOTECA AMBROSIANA, MILAN

BASILICA OF ST. JOHN LATERAN, ROME

Only a fragment remains of a fresco ascribed to Giotto, which shows Pope Boniface VIII proclaiming the Jubilee Year, 1300. However, a manuscript illustration *(top)* done in 1622 is believed to be based on the entire original fresco. The strong characterization of the Pope and a cardinal (at his right) in the fragment and the balanced composition of the crowd in the copy support the traditional belief that Giotto was the author of the work.

who paid it. Edward replied by threatening to have his sheriffs seize the temporal property of the Church anywhere in his kingdom. Philip's answer was to ban the export of all gold, silver and jewels, thus cutting off their flow from French church collections into the papal treasury. Boniface backed down, but not for long.

When he reopened fire, he concentrated it on the French King—ironically, the grandson of the saintly Louis IX whom the papacy a few decades earlier had invited to take over the Hohenstaufen domains in Italy. Philip IV, more commonly called Philip the Fair because opinion held him to be "the handsomest man in Europe," was an arrogant man, as nettlesome as Boniface, and more of a master of vitriol. In one exchange between them, the Pope wrote: "Let no one persuade you that you have no superior, and are not subordinate to the supreme authority of the Church. . . . He who thinks so is a fool . . . ; he who stubbornly affirms so is an infidel." Philip unhesitatingly rapped back: "To Boniface who gives himself out as Supreme Pontiff, little or no greeting. . . . Let your great fatuousness know that We are subject to no one in the affairs of this world. . . . Whosoever believes to the contrary We declare to be a fool and a madman."

Amid the salvos, Boniface decided to hold a huge celebration in Rome to mark the new centenary of Christ's birth—the event commemorated in Giotto's fresco. The response to the Jubilee of 1300 was overwhelming. From every corner of Europe some 200,000 people poured into the city, weary of the old century, hopeful of the new, drawn by the Pope's promise of a remission of punishment for their sins if they paid 15 visits to the tombs of St. Peter and St. Paul. Boniface offered the same reward to Roman citizens for 30 visits, and to foreigners who could not make the pilgrimage if they contributed the amount of the traveling expenses. The press of the crowds moving across the Tiber between the churches of the apostles required two-way traffic to be set up on the bridge of Sant' Angelo; the scene was one that Dante would later put to use in describing the passage of sinners to and fro in his *Infernno*.

Offerings heaped on the altars at St. Peter's and St. Paul's kept two priests busy night and day, one chronicler reported, "raking together infinite money." Thousands cheered whenever the exultant Boniface appeared before them, usually in papal vestments—but sometimes in imperial robes, exclaiming: "I am Caesar! I am Emperor!"

The Jubilee's immense success, and a defeat suffered by Philip in 1302 in a battle with Flemish rebels against his regime, encouraged the Pope to believe that final victory over the French monarch was within his grasp. He issued a bull that made the most sweeping papal claims to temporal supremacy in all Church history. "We declare, state, define and pronounce," Boniface wrote, "that it is altogether necessary to salvation for every human creature to be subject to the Roman pontiff."

Philip reacted by mounting a campaign to depose Boniface and bring this "monster with the double crown" to France to stand trial for heresy, idolatry, soothsaying and other alleged crimes. The King's emissary, joined by Italian foes of the Pope and a posse of troops, broke in on Boniface one morning in September 1303 in his bedroom at his family's palace at Anagni. He was kept captive for three days, but was finally rescued by townsfolk and returned to Rome in the custody of professed friends. He stayed in seclusion, a virtual hostage, and within a month died, fighting to the end; it was said that he tried to scratch out the eyes of anyone who came near him.

The next Pope, Benedict XI, was a peaceable man who tried to placate Philip, but he died within a year, shortly after eating a dish of figs; people took it as a matter of fact that the French had poisoned him. The next year, 1305, Philip tasted his sweetest triumph. The College of Cardinals elected a Frenchman, who reigned as Clement V without ever setting foot in Rome. The little town of Avignon in Provence, conveniently close to Philip, became the new seat of the papacy. It was to remain so for 70 years.

Turning-points are better seen in retrospect. Viewing the humiliation of Boniface, the brief tenure of Benedict and the accession of Clement, few Italians immediately realized that the Church was plunging to an all-time low in power and prestige. Only later was the absence of the popes from Rome labeled the Babylonian Captivity, in analogy to the exile of the ancient Jews from Palestine. But in the first disruptive years after the Jubilee of 1300, Italians, while uneasy, were still hopeful. None would have believed that the popes would knuckle under to France for long. Despite his nationality, even Clement was said to be hostile to Philip. After all, he had won his first high promotion—Archbishop of Bordeaux—from Boniface himself. He was expected soon to take up the traditional residence at the Lateran.

Well before this hope faded, however, an adjustment to the new order appeared in the making. The city-states of Italy had other vital concerns. Except for the perennially inflammable nobles, people in general had had their fill of fighting, inside their walls or out. They wanted stability. The middle class yearned to pursue its business dealings without the restraints of warfare.

Florence in particular had gone through convulsive times—thanks partly to Boniface. Control of the city, and of all Tuscany, had figured in his plans to bestride the world. Insufficiently distracted by his troubles with Philip, he had abetted the Blacks of Florence in their efforts to oust the relatively democratic government of the Whites. Indeed, during one rare truce with Philip he had arranged for the King's younger brother, Charles of Valois, to intervene in Florence, ostensibly as a conciliator. Charles rode into the city in November 1301—unarmed, as Dante was bitterly to write, "save with the lance of treachery wherewith Judas tilted." The Blacks soon fell upon the Whites in a paroxysm of violence unimagined even in lusty Florence. In the wholesale banishment of the vanquished that followed, Dante, a prominent target as a onetime member of a White priorate, was warned that if he ever came back to the city he would be burned alive.

The death of Boniface failed to dislodge the pro-papal Blacks, and it was under their regime that Giotto resumed his life in Florence. From their standpoint his credentials were impeccable. He, in turn, tended to his art, ever thriving, ever busy. By now he had an impressive number

MUSÉE DU LOUVRE, PARIS

This panel painting, showing St. Francis receiving the stigmata, is one of only three works that bear Giotto's name (it is lettered on the frame). The work was probably painted by Giotto's studio, with the master's name added so that it would bring a fair price. Both the style and content of the painting bear a striking resemblance to the St. Francis frescoes at Assisi. Compare the lower left-hand panel here with the scene on page 94.

of mouths to feed. Precisely when he had married Ciuta di Lapo del Pela, a girl from the Santa Reparata quarter of Florence, is uncertain; nor does any hint survive of her personality or background. They had eight children, four boys and four girls. One son was to become a painter, and a daughter was to marry one. Another son was to become the rector of a church in the Mugello, the district of his father's birth, another daughter a nun.

Other than these meager details, very little is known of Giotto's private life. Presumably his marriage was happy, for he seems to have taken his family with him on out-of-town commissions that called for protracted absences from home. The story is told that when he was painting the Arena Chapel at Padua, he was visited by Dante, now a rootless wanderer. Apparently some of Giotto's youngsters were underfoot, and Dante observed that they had inherited their father's looks. How was it, the poet asked, that a man who painted such beautiful pictures had produced such homely children? Giotto, who had an incurably ribald streak, took no offense. The answer, he said, was simple: "I make my pictures by day, and my babies by night."

Another side of Giotto's wit is revealed in an anecdote of his encounter with a courtier of Pope Benedict XI. According to this story, Benedict wanted to pursue his predecessor's plans for decorating St. Peter's, and dispatched an agent to visit the workshops of Tuscan artists and bring back samples of their skill. That the man included the renowned Giotto among his interviewees may have been due to an excess of zeal; in any event, he appeared one day on the doorstep of Giotto's workshop in Florence.

Conceit was never one of Giotto's failings; one encomium after his death, by the writer Boccaccio, noted that he did not even like to be called master. When Benedict's messenger explained his mission, Giotto listened gravely. Then, with an amused glint, he took a piece of paper and a brush dipped in red paint and, holding his arm close to his side in the manner of a compass, drew a perfect circle. Handed this work, the visitor registered alarm; he could scarcely pass along such a mockery to the Pope. As Vasari reconstructed the dialogue, the envoy asked: "Am I to have no other design but this?" Giotto reassured him: "It is enough and more than enough. Send it in with the others and you will see if it obtains recognition." The prediction proved true. Benedict relished the perfection of Giotto's performance.

The story spread far and wide, and gave currency to a new saying: "You are rounder than Giotto's 'O.'" This was a play on words; *tondo,* the Italian for round, also means simple. As for Benedict, he promptly put Giotto to work. It was during Benedict's eight-month papacy, Vasari reported, that Giotto painted the five frescoes of the life of Christ for the choir of old St. Peter's and a picture for the sacristy, an effort that earned him the handsome fee of 600 gold ducats.

While thus maintaining his contacts with Rome, Giotto was also engaged, during the opening years of the 14th Century, on a number of commissions in his hometown. Among them was a panel painting that bears his name, in Latin: *Opus Jocti Florentini,* the work of Giotto the

Florentine. Only two more works with his name attached survive; the time had not yet come when artists routinely signed works to proclaim their authorship.

The first of these paintings, *St. Francis Receiving the Stigmata,* now hangs in the Louvre, part of the booty of Napoleon's sweep through Italy. Its main scene and the three small scenes below strikingly resemble four frescoes of the St. Francis cycle at Assisi, in which the saint is shown acquiring the marks of stigmatization, shoring up the Church according to a dream of Pope Innocent III, winning papal sanction for the rules of his order, and preaching to the birds. Comparing the panel scenes and the corresponding Assisi frescoes, experts in iconography— the study of symbolic meanings in pictorial images—have concluded that the Louvre painting must have derived from the Assisi works. One notable example of an iconographical link appears in the scene of Innocent's dream: to represent the falling Church which Francis supports, the painter in both cases used a building easily recognizable to Italians of the time—the Lateran Basilica.

How well the painting was derived from the frescoes is another matter. Many scholars have judged it a mediocre effort, done in large part by Giotto's assistants; they believe that he signed it simply to assert his "commercial responsibility" for the work. But some experts also attach other significance to the signature. They cite it as proof that Giotto painted the Assisi cycle, arguing that he never would have affixed his name to the panel if it had been just a copy of another painter's work.

Originally the panel was ordered for and hung over the altar of the church of San Francesco in Pisa. Giotto evidently did not go there to paint it, but began and finished it in Florence, and had it carted the 50 miles to the seaport town. His own city was making demands on his time. For the church of San Giorgio alla Costa, he painted a *Virgin and Child Enthroned,* since badly damaged, and a *Crucifixion,* since lost. For the church of the Badia, built by Arnolfo di Cambio, he painted a polyptych for the main altar and a fresco cycle on the walls around it. For centuries they, too, were written off as lost. But just within the past few decades—in the kind of dramatic discovery that stirs hope eternal in questing scholars—both the missing altarpiece and fragments of the frescoes have been found.

The triumphant discoverer was Ugo Procacci, during World War II the man charged with the safe hiding of Florence's art treasures (and later appointed the city's Superintendent of Galleries). At the church of Santa Croce one day in 1940 he noticed a small yellowed sticker on the back of a polyptych of five panels that workmen were carrying away. On the label were inked the words *Estratto dalla --dia di Firenze,* removed from the *--dia* of Florence. Procacci deduced that this was Giotto's Badia altarpiece, mentioned by both Ghiberti and Vasari.

Analyzing the handwriting, Procacci concluded that the work had been removed from the church of the Badia in the Napoleonic occupation of 1810, and had later been installed, by error, at Santa Croce. A postwar restoration completed in 1958 stripped off layers of paint applied by artists after Giotto; a top section that had been added, disguising the original gabled tops of the panels, was cut away. The altarpiece emerged as Giotto had conceived it, about five feet high and 11 feet wide, showing the Madonna and Child flanked on the left by St. Nicholas and St. John, on the right by St. Peter and St. Benedict, each against a bright gold background. The work is in almost perfect condition.

This first find led Procacci to his second. The altarpiece seemed too big to be suitable for the present site of the main altar at the Badia. Studying old records, he found that this site was not the original one; it had been changed in a major reconstruction of 1628. The two walls at the sides of the original altar had been knocked down. So had the right half of the rear wall; but the left half had simply been covered up by a new inner wall.

Full investigation had to await the war's end and, following that, the disposal of more pressing peacetime problems. Finally, in October 1958, while the altarpiece was being restored, money was allocated to support the search for the frescoes and permission to go ahead was granted. Procacci had a mason carefully chisel out a small chink high up on the left rear wall, then mounted a tall ladder and put his hand through the hole. "I felt the original wall," he recalled. "It had a smooth surface, so I knew it had to be frescoed, since wall surfaces are normally rough." He shone a flashlight through the chink and saw that there was a little color. "My heart skipped a beat," he said.

The dismantling of the inner wall was gingerly begun. Six months later the old wall stood revealed, a sight both disappointing and enchanting. All but one head in the frescoes had been cut out in the 1628 renovation; the frescoes themselves had been damaged, or faded by time. But what fragments remain are testimony of the master's touch. Three scenes, all based on the life of the Virgin, are identifiable: an *Annunciation,* a *Presentation in the Temple* and *Joachim among the Shepherds.* In this scene is the one head that was not cut out, a profile of a gentle young shepherd, wearing a cowl. Behind him are a ram and two sheep.

Procacci has expressed optimism about future discoveries. "It is my great hope," he has said, "that somewhere, sometime, in some part of the world, the missing faces will turn up."

An indeterminate number of other paintings by Giotto have fallen victim to the attrition of time; early accounts mention at least a dozen works, some of ambitious scope, that have disappeared without a trace. But by some miracle, his greatest masterpiece—the frescoing of the entire interior of the Arena Chapel in Padua—has endured. The chapel has defied not only the onslaught of more than six centuries but a World War II aerial bombing of the city that wrecked a church just a few hundred yards away. Except for the necessary ministrations of restorers, Giotto's magnum opus remains as he painted it, sometime between 1305 and 1310.

Padua, 25 miles from Venice, was a new field for Giotto to conquer, as far north as he had yet traveled. His fame had preceded him. Paduans prided themselves on their cosmopolitanism. They had a university that was by then 83 years old, celebrated for its teaching of medicine and

This crest, belonging to the wealthy Scrovegni family of Padua, shows a rampant, pregnant sow, or *scrofa,* a possible root of the family name. In his *Inferno* the poet Dante described a figure "who on his wallet white, showed a blue sow in farrow"; it was obvious to Dante's contemporaries that the man was the miserly Reginaldo Scrovegni, who had died screaming, "Give me the keys of my strongbox so that no one may get my money." Scrovegni was denied Christian burial because he was a usurer, and Dante consigned him unhesitatingly to hell.

law. They had perhaps the liveliest intellectual community in Italy. Through their commercial ties with the Venetians they also had affluence.

Giotto's patron in Padua, Enrico degli Scrovegni, was a scion of a family addicted to money-making. This zest for finance had tarnished the Scrovegni image. Enrico's father, Reginaldo, had practiced usury so blatant that the Church had denied him a Christian burial, thus also tying up his estate. Enrico was never a popular citizen and his involvement with Paduan culture was limited. His chief extracurricular interest was the *Cavalieri Gaudenti,* the merry knights, a noble order given to revelry under the cloak of devotion to pious works. But he was shrewd if not profound. When he decided to build a chapel his avowed aim was to atone for his father's sins. At the same time such a move could not help but improve his own public relations. Besides, he was more or less obliged to build the chapel. The Bishop of Padua had made it plain that this would be a quid pro quo for the release of part of his father's funds, which Enrico needed to decorate a palatial residence.

As it turned out, he achieved none of his purposes. The palace, a sumptuous edifice that was to be a showplace of Padua until its demolition in 1820, was his to enjoy but briefly. A decade or so after the chapel was consecrated in March 1305, he was driven out of the city in a major political upheaval; he returned only in death, to be interred, at his request, in the chapel's apse. His attempt to refurbish his father's name also failed, for at about the time that he went into involuntary exile in Venice, Dante's *Divine Comedy* fixed Reginaldo's sinister reputation forevermore by consigning him to the seventh circle of Hell.

Yet out of the mixed motives that impelled Enrico degli Scrovegni to build a chapel and commission the great Giotto to decorate it came a work of art of marvelous purity *(pages 112-129),* so lucid and straightforward in its expression of human joy and sorrow, weakness and strength, that it has never since ceased to stir wonder.

The Arena Chapel, so called because it stands on the site of an ancient Roman amphitheater, is a narrow, pinkish brick building just 67 feet long. The exterior is undistinguished and scarcely prepares the visitor for the glories to be found within. From the inside, however, one fact becomes quickly apparent: there is a remarkable harmony between the simple architecture and the painting on its walls.

Giotto's grand plan for the interior included three tiers of frescoes, 34 in all, along the chapel's side walls; the topmost tier is devoted to scenes of the early life of the Virgin, the middle tier to scenes of the childhood and ministry of Christ, and the third to scenes of His Passion. A single fresco of the Last Judgment covers the entrance wall. Directly opposite it, over an arched doorway leading to the sanctuary, is a scene depicting God the Father sending the angel Gabriel on his mission. Below, flanking the doorway, are four smaller frescoes, two of which portray the Annunciation—in the left panel Gabriel bringing the word and in the right panel the Virgin receiving it. This is the scene that greets the spectator as he enters, at once proclaiming that the chapel honors the Virgin Annunciate.

Overhead, on a barrel-vaulted ceiling of blue studded with gold

BIBLIOTECA DEL MUSEO CIVICO, PADUA

This engraving, made in 1842, shows the Arena Chapel to the right of an older palace, which Enrico Scrovegni, Reginaldo's son, bought and redecorated. The chapel's portico was added after Giotto's time; his picture of the building *(page 100)* does not show it. Before the engraving was made (from an earlier watercolor), the palace had already been torn down, and the chapel, in bad repair, was in danger of being demolished by its new owner. But in 1880 the chapel and grounds were purchased by the citizens of Padua and preserved as an artistic monument.

stars, Giotto painted 10 medallions of Christ, Mary and the Prophets. Along the lower part of the walls, forming a plinthlike base reminiscent of a Classical monument, he placed 14 allegorical figures of the Virtues and Vices *(end papers),* each facing its opposite number. Painted in monochrome against a background colored to resemble marble, these figures look more like bas-reliefs than two-dimensional representations. They are among the major triumphs of the chapel.

Added to all this, between the frescoes on the side walls, are painted numerous decorative motifs and vignettes of Scriptural themes. Very little wall space is unfilled, yet Giotto's genius has accomplished an impression of total order, clarity and serenity.

The masterly arrangement of the whole is matched in its parts. In each of the three rows of frescoes on the side walls the scenes unfold in sequence, beginning at the right of the arched doorway and ending at the left of the doorway. The top frescoes, for example, start with a scene showing the rejection of the sacrificial offering of Joachim, the Virgin's father-to-be, because he is childless. Other frescoes show Joachim and Anna, his wife, being separately informed that they will have a daughter, and the couple's reunion at the city gate. On the opposite wall, the scenes on the top tier continue with the birth and childhood of the Virgin and her betrothal and marriage, ending at a logical point in the chronology, the Annunciation scene flanking the arched doorway. The story picks up directly below to show the Virgin's meeting with Elizabeth, the mother-to-be of John the Baptist; the middle row of frescoes then takes up the scenes of Christ's birth and life. With consummate skill, Giotto made it easy for the spectator to read the story by a horizontal arrangement of figures within each scene, so that the eye moves naturally from one episode to the next.

In the hands of a lesser artist, the calculated organization of the frescoes might have seemed cold and contrived. The brilliance of Giotto's feat lay in his blending of order and high drama. He knew, unerringly, the point he wished to make in each scene. He made it with utmost economy, yet with the greatest expressiveness. Faces, glances, gestures, postures bespeak some authentic emotion, whether the quiet joy and tender care with which Mary places the Infant Jesus in the manger in the *Nativity,* or the cruel gleams in the eyes of Christ's tormentors in the *Flagellation.*

Indeed, it is through the individual figures that the drama of the Arena frescoes comes through most strongly. The scholar Richard Offner noted that "Giotto's concern here was with establishing the dignity of human fate through the material significance of the human figure." And this is nowhere as evident as in the episodes showing Joachim and Anna, and the events that precede the Virgin's birth.

Perhaps the most beautiful and convincing of these scenes is *Joachim's Dream (page 118).* In it, the disconsolate Joachim, who has been driven away by a priest of his temple because he is childless, has ashamedly retreated into the mountains to pray and fast, with only a small hut to shelter him. There, in a natural setting that Giotto creates with the simplest of painted shapes and details—a craggy tower of rock whose

ARENA CHAPEL, PADUA

Compensating for an asymmetrical arrangement of windows in the Arena Chapel, Giotto designed ingenious decorative borders like this one to fill out spaces between frescoes and allow him to present his scenes in an orderly and logical manner. Each of these painted strips contains a medallion with a symbolic scene *(opposite page)* that helps to carry the story forward.

forbidding outline is broken only by a single tree and the austere, slatted cubicle of the hut—the isolated figure of Joachim withdraws within himself. Giotto pictures the man asleep on the ground, his body slumped forward, with his bearded head cradled on an arm propped up by a bended knee. Joachim is as enveloped in a dream as he is literally wrapped in his robe.

Across from Joachim stand the shepherds, gentle men who seek to comfort him, to offer solace. One of them leans forward on his crook, a hand tentatively raised as if loath to break in on the dreamer.

The final element in the scene is the figure of an angel. This wonderful creation, standing out starkly against the blue sky, might have intruded or drawn attention away from the central figure, Joachim. But Giotto pictures him without fuss as he gently descends toward the dreaming man, helping to focus further attention on him. Indeed, it is only the second shepherd's skyward glance that seems to give confirmation to the angel's presence. Giotto has allowed nothing to detract from the story that he is telling, and although that story requires that the angel be there, he makes certain that the viewer knows his function. He is coming to tell Joachim that he may return to the city, that a blessed child is to be born to him. The scholar Cesare Gnudi, who believes that Giotto painted these bare, simple scenes first, suggests that the "poem" of the whole fresco cycle begins in these early, stately cadences.

Under Giotto's brush the stories of the sacred personages of Christianity became stories of all mankind. Among the sources that he probably drew upon were the Old and New Testaments, folk legends, a variety of earlier portrayals in paint, mosaic and stone and numerous written apocryphal accounts of the lives of the Holy Family. But these sources served only as springboard. Giotto alone could provide the power of picturization, the expression of emotion, and the genre touches with which the viewer could identify: Anna's sullen maid seated at her spinning wheel, the inquisitive townswomen hovering near Joachim and Anna at the Golden Gate to share their good news, the porcine feaster at the marriage at Cana.

Figuratively as well as literally underlying the narrative scenes, Giotto's Virtues and Vices sum up the human character in all its basic elements. Ranged on the left side, turning toward the damned in the Last Judgment fresco, are the personifications of human frailty; opposite are the personifications of human nature at its best. Folly is a grotesque clown in a feathered headdress. Wrath is a disheveled woman tearing at her clothes. Idolatry is a helmeted figure, eyes shaded and ears covered, who is holding a small idol. Envy, a serpent issuing from her mouth, claws a purse. Fortitude holds a shield against which arrows fall, blunted. Faith holds a cross and a scroll inscribed with the Creed. Charity bears a bowl of fruit and flowers, Temperance a sheathed sword. Justice holds her scales in balance. She alone, of all Giotto's figures, wears a crown.

At the Arena Chapel, art magnificently fulfills its function as an experience to be shared. Italy was not to see a work of equal scope and impact until Michelangelo's Sistine Chapel frescoes two centuries later.

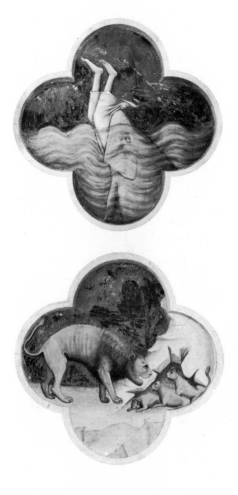

These medallions in the Arena Chapel flank the fresco that pictures the dead Christ in Mary's arms and relate it to the Resurrection scene that follows. The Jonah and the Whale medallion (*top*) suggests the miracle of resurrection as does the one showing a lion with cubs—a reference to a popular medieval belief that lions are born dead and have life breathed into them three days later.

The Arena Chapel

In 1305, Giotto began painting the commission that was to be his greatest achievement: the completely frescoed interior of the newly built Arena Chapel in Padua, erected on the site of a Roman amphitheater. The work was financed by Enrico Scrovegni, a wealthy Paduan whose father had amassed a fortune by lending money at exorbitant rates of interest. Indeed, Dante, in his *Divine Comedy,* had consigned the elder Scrovegni to Hell among the usurers; it was later said that Enrico defended his family name against a verse by Dante with a church by Giotto.

Compared to the more ornate Gothic interiors common to the era, the building Enrico ordered was a mural painter's dream. A simple rectangle, roofed by a single barrel vault, it had no inside pilasters, cornices, ribs or moldings; only six windows on one side broke the 134-foot-long expanse of otherwise smooth walls. The architecture presented Giotto with few restrictions in the size, shape or number of his paintings, and he organized them brilliantly.

The 40 major frescoes in the chapel tell the stories of the early life of the Virgin and the life of Christ. Working in a supremely economical style and with a dazzling sense of drama and pace, Giotto treated the viewer to charming details like the one at right, as he carried his narrative from painting to painting through the spiritual history of man's redemption.

In a detail from *The Adoration of the Magi (scene 18, page 120),* Giotto emphasized the joy at Christ's birth with such particulars as the face of a spirited camel. This lively note contrasts sharply with the quiet adoration of the kings, demonstrating Giotto's unusual skill in portraying specific and appropriate emotions.

OVERLEAF: The interior of the Arena Chapel, looking toward *The Last Judgment* on the entrance wall.

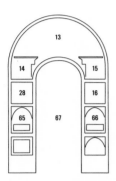

The Triumphal Arch

A key to Giotto's frescoes

Giotto's narrative in the Arena Chapel is divided into three sequences arranged in horizontal bands around the walls. The top row *(scenes 1-12 in the diagram)* depicts the early life of the Virgin. The middle row *(scenes 17-27)* illustrates the early life of Christ; it actually begins in scenes 13-16 on the Triumphal Arch *(small diagram at left)*, which faces the visitor as he enters the chapel through the door beneath scene 40. *The Passion of Christ*, which begins in scene 28 on the arch, is concluded in the bottom row *(scenes 29-39)*. Like the others, this sequence proceeds clockwise, returning to the arch, which encloses the altar.

Each narrative scene is pictured on the pages that follow with a number relating it to the diagram above (and to the photograph on the preceding pages). The complete list at left also identifies the medallions on the ceiling *(scenes 41-50)*, which depict prophets, and the band of figures around the base of the walls *(scenes 51-64)*, which symbolize virtues and vices. The largest scene of all *(40)*, appropriately, is *The Last Judgment*, which confronts the viewer as he turns to leave the chapel.

The Life of Mary

1 *The Expulsion of Joachim from the Temple*

2 *Joachim Retires to the Sheepfold*

3 *The Annunciation to Anna*

4 *The Sacrifice of Joachim*

5 *The Vision of Joachim*

6 *The Meeting at the Golden Gate*

7 *The Birth of the Virgin*

8 *The Presentation of the Virgin in the Temple*

9 *The Presentation of the Rods*

10 *The Watching of the Rods*

11 *The Betrothal of the Virgin*

12 *The Virgin's Return Home*

The Vision of Joachim (scene 5)

Giotto's direct and lucid style is especially evident in the early episodes
of his narrative, which tell the story of Joachim and Anna, the Virgin's
parents. Joachim, driven out of the temple because he is childless, has gone into
the wilderness to fast and pray for 40 days and nights; in the scene above,
he has fallen asleep and in a dream an angel comes to announce that his
wife Anna is at last going to have a child.

Giotto has painted the sleeping Joachim as a compact, passive form, wrapped
in the folds of a simple robe. Yet he is unquestionably the emotional center of
the scene. Other elements—the angel's gesture, the stance of the shepherd in
the foreground—draw the viewer's eye in the direction of the somnolent man
and neither the sparely drawn landscape nor the hut distract attention.
Following this scene, a joyous Joachim returns to the city and greets Anna in a
warm embrace *(detail at right)*.

Detail from *The Meeting at the Golden Gate (scene 6)*

The Life of Christ

Flanking the top of the chapel's Triumphal Arch, and marking the beginning of the second chapter of the narrative, are the angel Gabriel *(right)*, and the Virgin Mary *(far right)*; he is informing her that she will bear the Son of God. The angel's hand indicates the direction in which the story will flow. In this and other ways, Giotto carefully but unobtrusively points up the left-to-right movement of the dramatic line. Central figures like Christ in scene 27 gesture in such a way as to lead the eye toward the next episode. Even the donkeys in scenes 20 and 26 move the story along. Yet these signals, always appropriate to the action, never break a mood or detract from its meaning.

14 *The Archangel Gabriel*

16 *The Visitation*

17 *The Nativity*

18 *The Adoration of the Magi*

22 *Christ Disputing with the Elders*

23 *The Baptism of Christ*

24 *The Marriage at Cana*

15 *The Annunciate Virgin*

19 *The Presentation of Christ in the Temple*

20 *The Flight into Egypt*

21 *The Massacre of the Innocents*

25 *The Raising of Lazarus*

26 *The Entry into Jerusalem*

27 *The Expulsion of the Merchants from the Temple*

Detail from *The Massacre of the Innocents*
(*scene 21*)

In portraying the monstrous
slaughter of innocent children by
King Herod's soldiers, Giotto not
only demonstrated his grasp of
dramatic essentials but also
displayed his concern for rhythm,
for space-defining volumes and for
compositional balance.

The inclusion of this scene as an
episode in the life of Christ was
not unprecedented. Many other
painters and sculptors, including
Giovanni Pisano, had been
challenged by the drama of this
wanton attempt to kill the Infant
Christ. Though Giotto probably
knew some of the earlier
portrayals, his own was a new and
powerful expression of the story.
Unlike Giovanni, who made the
commanding Herod the focus of
his scene *(pages 50-51)*, Giotto
placed two murdering soldiers at
the center of the action *(detail at
right)*, drawing attention to the
repulsive deed itself. He opposed
the soldiers with a mass of pleading
women, who seem almost to
merge into one unit, and pulled
the groups together with the
lateral motion of the central
soldier's sword. The dead children
on the ground, who serve as a
base for the frieze of figures, further
emphasize the horror of the scene.

The Passion of Christ

In the final sequence in the Arena Chapel, depicting events from Christ's betrayal through the Pentecost, Giotto's expressive powers reached their peak. Here, even such relatively minor details as the angels from the *Pietà (detail, right; scene 36, below)* add to the emotional impact: their faces are contorted in a catalogue of grief. Compare these weeping figures with the joyous angels in the Nativity *(scene 17, page 120)*. Giotto used a landscape element —the single, leafless tree at the far right—to convey the tragedy, as though all nature were in mourning. But even here he did not simply paint a symbol; the tree is a natural element, carefully observed and drawn.

28 *The Pact of Judas*

29 *The Last Supper*

30 *The Washing of the Feet*

34 *The Road to Calvary*

35 *The Crucifixion*

36 *The Pietà*

Detail from the *Pietà (scene 36)*

31 *The Kiss of Judas*

32 *Christ before Caiaphas*

33 *The Mocking of Christ*

37 *The Angel at the Tomb and The Noli Me Tangere*

38 *The Ascension*

39 *The Pentecost*

Aﬅer building to an emotional climax in the *Pietà*, Giotto masterfully released the tension in the following scene *(37)* in which Christ arises from His tomb. All its details set a mood of peace and tranquillity, down to the sleeping soldiers who cannot see the miracle taking place in their presence *(detail below)*. Beneath a vast and empty sky, the figures are bathed in a dawn light, which softens the brilliant but harmonious colors that Giotto used.

Detail from *The Angel at the Tomb (scene 37)*

With *The Last Judgment,* a huge fresco covering the entire entrance wall of the chapel, Giotto provided a dramatic conclusion for his narrative of God and man. Here, Christ, flanked by His Apostles, sits enthroned above mankind, summoning the blessed to heaven with His right hand, and condemning the damned with His left. Below Him, Giotto shows Hell as a fiery chamber of horrors, in which the tiny, white-robed figure of Judas,

Christ's betrayer *(to the left of the monstrous Devil)* hangs for his crime. Among the blessed, Giotto painted himself *(fifth from the left in the bottom row at left)* and Enrico Scrovegni, the donor of the chapel *(presenting the model of it above the left side of the doorway).* High above the scene, flanking the window are two angels—one of them shown in the detail above—who literally roll back the heavens to reveal the gates of Paradise.

The Last Judgment (scene 40)

GALLERIA DEGLI UFFIZI, FLORENCE

VI

Strenuous Decades

Giotto was just about 40 when he scored his triumph at the Arena Chapel. Physically as well as creatively, it had called forth his fullest energies. A more egocentric artist might have chosen to rest awhile on his laurels. Giotto, however, seems to have considered his achievement simply as so much work completed. For someone of his practical bent, the rewards lay not in glory but in widened avenues to more work and hence more wealth. He had the countryman's esteem for both.

It was predictable that the Paduans would want more from the hand of the celebrated Florentine in their midst. Giotto undertook two other major commissions, neither destined to be as durable as his Arena frescoes, for two of the city's proudest landmarks: the basilica built in honor of its favorite saint, the miracle-working St. Anthony of Padua, and the communal Palazzo della Ragione, the "Palace of Reason," so called because any citizen could go there and plead his own cause by stating his reason for an alleged offense.

Both buildings were huge, a far cry from the modest simplicity of the Arena Chapel. The central feature of the Palazzo was an audience hall, the Salone, where Paduans went to seek justice; a room nearly 300 feet long, 90 feet wide, and about as high, it had a cavernous appearance emphasized by a ceiling shaped like an inverted boat. Giotto was but one of many painters who were to adorn this curious chamber; ultimately more than 300 frescoes would cover its walls.

The basilica, too, had its unusual aspects; structurally it appeared almost unplanned, a massive burst of fervor in brick and stone. The Paduans' passion for St. Anthony—a Franciscan of noble Portuguese birth who had spent less than two years among them—had fired them to begin the vast church in his name immediately upon his death in 1231. The task took some 70 years; the protracted construction resulted in an architectural hybrid, with Romanesque arches, a Gothic rose window, and Byzantine cupolas reminiscent of those atop the church of San Marco in nearby Venice. There were seven domes, each representing a miracle in which St. Anthony was said to have restored a corpse to life.

Shortly after the basilica was completed in 1307, Giotto was com-

The *Ognissanti Madonna* is so called because it was created by Giotto for the Church of All Saints (Ognissanti) in Florence. Painted shortly after the Arena Chapel frescoes, the panel painting shows Giotto's brilliant evocation of three-dimensional space in the solidly constructed throne and the static bulk of the Madonna figure.

Ognissanti Madonna, 1306-1310

missioned to paint a fresco in a small chapel near the sacristy that was used as the chapter room, or meeting place, of the Franciscan monks. Unfortunately, a hurricane, three fires, whitewashings and intermittent reconstructions have left Giotto's decorative ensemble for the chapel with only a pale glimmer of its past glory.

To the left of the entrance wall are two frescoes in the semicircular shape of lunettes. One, faded to little more than an outline, depicts the stigmatization of St. Francis, much as it was treated in the signed Giotto panel now in the Louvre. The other, somewhat better preserved, depicts the execution of five Franciscans at Ceuta in Morocco, at the order of the local Saracen prince. The Ceuta incident had been the turning point of St. Anthony's life; while a young monk in Portugal, he had met the Franciscans prior to their African journey, and it was the news of their martyrdom that had decided him on his own preaching mission.

On facing walls of the chapel, separated by painted pilasters, are eight single figures in niches. Among those still identifiable are St. Anthony, St. Francis, and St. Clare, the pious noblewoman of Assisi whom Francis inspired to found the order of nuns known as the Poor Clares. In all figures the marks of destructive dampness show in eroded faces and limbless bodies; bits and pieces here and there, including an enigmatic glimpse of part of a skeleton, trace the tragic pattern of fragmentation.

Early sources assert that Giotto concentrated his chief effort in this chapel on a series of scenes of the Passion of Christ. Not a scrap of them remains; presumably they were painted on the walls above the cornice, and were destroyed or removed when a new ceiling was put in place. The frescoes that survive pose the familiar problem of authorship; which parts were by Giotto himself, which by his assistants, and which by later restorers is a question that scholars consider beyond answer by now. The case for Giotto's own handiwork rests primarily on the figures on the end walls. Despite the buffetings they have endured, they retain a certain majestic monumentality that bespeaks the artist of the Arena Chapel.

The riddles of Giotto's frescoes at the basilica are as naught compared to those surrounding his work at the Palazzo della Ragione. At the right of the main entrance to its Salone, below a frescoed figure of an astronomer, is inscribed Giotto's name. Like some tiny artifact in a mammoth cave, the inscription is easily overlooked. Yet it is the sole (and undependable) vestige of Giotto's presence. Whatever he painted in the Salone has vanished—either incinerated in a fire that swept the Palazzo in 1420 or buried beneath layers of later frescoes.

The testimony of a contemporary chronicler and of later writers indicates that Giotto's achievement in the Salone was one of his most ambitious. Ghiberti described one part of it as an allegory on the Christian faith. As frustrated as Giotto's admirers may feel over the loss of this work, they grieve even more over another—believed to be Giotto's first large-scale venture into the field of secular painting. This was a fresco series representing the signs of the zodiac and the seven planets. The scholar Eugenio Battisti has suggested that it was intended as a "monumental horoscope" of Padua. No inkling exists as to how Giotto handled the theme, but there is a tradition that he relied on a text furnished by Pietro d'Abano, one of Padua's most learned men and possibly its most intriguing personality.

Pietro was a physician, magician, university professor and a translator of Aristotle; he was also the author in his own right of treatises on a variety of topics, from the classification of poisons to the reconciliation of the conflicting opinions of Greek, Latin, Hebrew and Arabic scholars on all the unsolved questions of human knowledge. But above all he was an astrologer, who believed that the movements of the stars and planets controlled man's life, health and eventual fate.

An inveterate traveler, Pietro journeyed as far as Paris and Constantinople. In 1306, when he was nearing 60, he came home to Padua and to his presumed collaboration with Giotto. Although the visible effects of this joint effort were to be erased, it presaged the bond that was increasingly to unite men of art and men of learning in the Renaissance.

Whatever Pietro's own horoscope foretold for him, a luckless end impended. In time he got into deep trouble with the Church. Padua was a hotbed of Averroism, a doctrine holding that there was a philosophic as well as a religious truth, and Pietro was its leading exponent. This unorthodox view inevitably forced the Church to act against him. However, when the Inquisition launched proceedings against Pietro, the charges centered not on his espousal of Averroism but on his alleged practice of black magic. He died during his trial in 1316, but was not allowed to rest in peace: his bones were burned in punishment for his heresy.

Giotto, presumably unaffected by the furor, pursued his busy career. For almost a decade after Padua, until about 1320, he touched base in Florence infrequently. As word spread of the splendors he had wrought in Padua, neighboring cities sought his services. Most of them were scarcely more than small towns, insular in their way of life, but no painter could resist one special advantage they offered: a breed of patron who had both unassailable authority and ample means.

This part of Italy was despot country, the stronghold of entrenched families in which rule was passed from father to son. Verona belonged to the della Scala family, Ferrara to the House of Este, Rimini to the Malatesta, Urbino to the Montefeltro, Ravenna to the da Polenta. Sometimes the leaders of these clans shored up their hereditary claims to control by obtaining papal or imperial appointment as "vicars" of the territories they governed; sometimes they went through the motions of securing popular consent. No one was really fooled. Each despot wielded absolute power over his tight little principality, and brooked none of the strivings toward self-government that stirred communities elsewhere. In lieu of liberty he provided prosperity, stability and order.

The 14th Century despot could be fearsome and capable, at once brutal toward his foes and generous to his friends. Both Can Grande della Scala in Verona and Guido da Polenta in Ravenna extended their hospitality to the homeless Dante. It may have been Dante who alerted them to the availability of his friend Giotto. They needed no urging. Like other despots in history, they saw in art a useful status symbol, present and future proof of their luster.

Giotto painted both in the palaces of the despots and in the major

TEMPIO MALATESTIANO, RIMINI

The poignant portrayal of Christ on this crucifix in Rimini bears strong resemblances to the one shown below, which Giotto is believed to have painted for the Arena Chapel after he completed his frescoes there. At some time in the past the traditional panels from the extremities of the Rimini crucifix were removed; only one has been recovered.

MUSEO CIVICO, PADUA

churches of their cities. This shuttling between the secular and the sacred was in itself a novel turn in his career, one about which scholars long to know more. But the chief source of information on Giotto's labors for his lordly patrons, Vasari's biography, is uncharacteristically terse on this score. Vasari named the churches—six in all—which Giotto decorated in Verona, Ferrara, Ravenna and Rimini, and noted also that he "did a few things" in Urbino. However, the account sheds little light on Giotto's specific works, religious or secular.

It does mention, in passing, a portrait of Can Grande. The implication is that this was a separate painting rather than an incidental feature of some fresco. If so, the work was a landmark of sorts, a pioneer step into the great field of formal portraiture that later Italians were to exploit with brilliant success. Giotto, of course, had already proved his hand at characterization, in the depiction of Enrico Scrovegni in the *Last Judgment* at the Arena Chapel, and in the painting of Pope Boniface announcing the Jubilee; he may even have included his own likeness in the crowd scenes of some of his frescoes.

But a distinctive portrait, conceived as such, was a different proposition, and an exciting one as well in the particular case of the Lord of Verona. Among the despots of his day, Can Grande was one of the most formidable, but he was a man whose lust for conquest was matched by his zeal for culture. When not raiding his neighbors' domains, he presided over a glittering court that held poets and painters and sculptors in high esteem; in this he was the prototype of such splendid Renaissance autocrats as Lodovico Sforza of Milan and Lorenzo de' Medici of Florence. It is tempting to speculate on what passed between Can Grande and Giotto during the portrait sessions, and whether famed sitter and famed painter chatted of war, or art, or perhaps of a recent local event that had agitated Verona—a tragedy of young love involving two proud families, which Shakespeare was to immortalize in *Romeo and Juliet* nearly three centuries later.

The fate of the portrait, and of just about everything else that Giotto produced in the five cities, is almost totally befogged. Scholars, by no means unanimously, attribute only two extant works to him. One, at Rimini, is a crucifix over 14 feet high, overwhelming in its austere grandeur. The figure of Christ is nearly identical with the one in a smaller crucifix, now in the museum at Padua, that once hung in the sanctuary of the Arena Chapel. The Rimini crucifix adorns one of the city's architectural treasures: the Tempio Malatestiano, a "temple of fame" built around 1450 at the behest of the murderous Sigismondo Malatesta, a descendant of the despot for whom Giotto worked. The Tempio's renowned architect, Leone Battista Alberti, designed it as a Renaissance-style shell to enclose the old church of San Francesco—one of the six churches cited by Vasari as a scene of Giotto's labors.

The second work ascribed to Giotto is a ceiling fresco in another church on Vasari's list, San Giovanni Evangelista in Ravenna. The fresco is rectangular in shape, divided diagonally into four segments with a medallion at the center. In each of the compartments one of the four Evangelists faces one of the four learned Doctors of the Church, shown reading, writing, or meditating. All eight figures are much retouched; those who argue for Giotto's authorship base the claim mainly on the manifest skill with which the potential clutter of a complex theme has been turned into a well-ordered harmony.

A number of other churches, notably in Ravenna, have staked a claim to Giotto. But the scholarly consensus holds that the works they advance as his prove only that there were numerous aspiring imitators among the local painters of his time. Giotto's impact on regional style long outlived his visit.

When Giotto left Ravenna, Vasari recorded, he was "laden" with riches, and presumably he reaped no less from the open-handed despots of the other cities. By now Giotto was a very wealthy man, more in a class with the flourishing capitalists of Florence than with the merely prosperous master-painters. In addition to a large workshop, operated when he was out of town by those assistants who did not travel with him, he owned property in Florence and in the surrounding countryside. Then as now, land was regarded as an attractive investment, and Giotto bought up a number of tracts in his native valley of the Mugello.

Legal documents in the Florentine archives indicate that he applied as sharp an eye to his economic interests as to his painting commissions. They record Giotto as leasing a house to one man, renting out a piece of land to another, authorizing his son Francesco to act as his agent in various transactions, specifying a suitable dowry for his daughter Chiara in a marriage contract. When he felt the need, Giotto never hesitated to resort to litigation, whether in large matters or small. He waged a battle with a notary over the disputed possession of some acreage in the Mugello, and he proved equally stubborn in a skirmish involving the modest sum of two florins.

As recounted by the chronicler Franco Sacchetti, the latter incident was provoked by a bumpkin who came to Giotto's workshop and left a shield to be painted with his "coat of arms." More amused than annoyed, Giotto decided on a design that would show the shield "armed to the teeth." He had an assistant bedeck it with representations of a sword, lance, dagger, cuirass, gorget, helmet, armlets, gauntlets and leg-pieces. The customer denounced the result as rubbish. Giotto retorted: "You scarcely know who you are yourself should anyone ask you; yet you come here and say to me, 'Paint my arms.' If you had been one of the Bardi, that might have been enough. . . . Whence came you? Who were your ancestors? . . . Go into the world a little, before you talk of arms as if you were the Duke of Bavaria." The man sued Giotto for "spoiling" his shield. Giotto countered with a suit for payment of two florins—and collected.

The story is the more interesting for its incidental insight into Giotto's social outlook. He had come a long way from his own rustic beginnings. Popes, despots, plutocratic families like the Bardi—for whom he was soon to paint a chapel—all gave him welcome. By hard work and prudent investment he had acquired wealth, and with it a touch of impatience at those who aspired higher than their rank but who neither could nor would, as he put it, "go into the world a little." In his paintings he was capable of expressing a deep compassion for his fellow beings; yet he could drive some exceedingly hard bargains with those less fortunate than himself.

One of his lucrative sidelines was built up on the inability of men of more modest means to repay the debts they had incurred. A petty trader might seek a loan from a creditor, offering some possession as security. Giotto would guarantee the loan's repayment. Then, if the debtor defaulted, Giotto would pay the creditor and take over whatever the debtor had put up as security, usually worth much more than the loan. If he had to hound the man, there were *procuratori* (lawyers) to help; records show that in 1314 alone Giotto was employing six such aides.

Another source of profit lay in the plight of the weavers of Florence. There was a division of labor in the city's textile industry into some 20 clothmaking and finishing processes. Some functions, notably spinning and weaving, were handled by workers at home. The employer's agent would bring wool to the spinners—mostly women of nearby villages —then later pick up the spun yarn and turn it over to the city-dwelling weavers. These men, totally at the mercy of the textile magnates, were forbidden by city law to organize in any way, and were paid on a piecework basis at bare subsistence rates. They also had to supply their own equipment, and since they could ill afford to buy looms, they were forced to hire them at exorbitant rentals, either from their employers or from alert entrepreneurs. Giotto was one of these. Since the rental device circumvented the church ban on usury, his profit sometimes ran higher than 100 per cent.

The stark contrast between the theory of universal brotherhood preached by St. Francis, and the practice of it, apparently left Giotto undisturbed. He shared this indifference with virtually all well-to-do Florentines; few felt moved to ponder the lot of the downtrodden. Among the exceptions were the members of a monastic order known as the Frati Umiliati, or the Humble Brethren. Motivated both by a desire for the simple life of sheep-raising and a solicitude for the welfare of the poor, the Umiliati had effectively combined these concerns in a network of thriving sheep farms and a training school for textile skills, an important adjunct to the Florentine industry.

The paths of Giotto and the Umiliati may have crossed in the pursuit of their common, if antipathetic, interest in the textile workers. Out of the proceeds of wool-growing the Umiliati had built the church of the Ognissanti (All Saints) in Florence, and they commissioned Giotto to decorate it. Among the crowds of lowly worshipers who viewed his works, there must certainly have been men from whom he had wrung a profit. He gave them in turn a feast for the eyes and, in the case of one work—a powerful painting of the Madonna *(page 130)*—balm for the spirit as well.

A huge single panel that served as an altarpiece, Giotto's *Ognissanti Madonna* is now in the Uffizi Gallery, in the company of Cimabue's *Trinita Madonna* and Duccio's *Rucellai Madonna.* The similarity of format is evident. In Giotto's painting as in the other two, the Virgin, holding the Christ Child, sits enthroned and attended by angels. In one sense

MUSEO DELL'OPERA DEL DUOMO, FLORENCE

Arnolfo di Cambio's Madonna and Child was one of the many statues he designed and carved for the façade of Florence's Duomo, the Cathedral on which he also served as master architect. Arnolfo's brilliant work so pleased the Florentine Council that two years before his death in 1302, they voted to remit all his taxes. His sculptural style, evident in the solid, solemn presence of this figure, influenced Giotto when, several years later, the painter created a Madonna *(page 130)* for Florence's Church of All Saints.

the work is a synthesis. Giotto's Madonna, possessed of neither beauty nor charm, is in the elemental, massive mold of Cimabue's. Giotto's angels, on the other hand, owe a debt to Duccio. Two of them kneel, holding flower-filled vases; two stand, one proffering a crown and the other the oil of anointment. The four figures signal something new in Giotto's art, an awakening interest in elegance and grace; plainly he had looked long and hard at the work of his Sienese contemporary, the closest contender he had for primacy in the painting field. Moreover, Giotto had drawn on still another master, Arnolfo di Cambio, who had carved a similarly majestic Madonna and Child a decade or so earlier for the façade of the Florence Cathedral.

For all this, the *Ognissanti Madonna* is a work of strong originality. Giotto might synthesize, but he could not avoid leaving his own unique imprint. He was probing intensively in this work, seeking fuller command of the fundamental problem of planting credible forms in credible space. The extent to which he succeeded makes the painting a major achievement in Western art. Renaissance masters would find their task easier because of Giotto's explorations.

By adding steps to the Madonna's throne, and opening its sides so that the faces of saints standing in the background of the scene show through them, Giotto made the throne seem a fully three-dimensional structure. By distributing lights and darks, he made the Madonna herself seem as palpable as the space around her. As Bernard Berenson noted: "Our tactile imagination is put to play immediately." For the first time in Italian painting, the Madonna is painted with all the attributes of a womanly figure. The contours of her limbs are accentuated by the flow of her robe and further emphasized by the weight of the Christ Child upon her lap; the material of her blouse pulls against the swell of her bosom. Furthermore, in making the Madonna figure almost uncontainable within the niche of the throne, Giotto added to the impression of bodily substance.

Giotto's Madonna does not gaze at her Child. She holds Him much as the crowned figure of Justice in the Arena Chapel holds her scales; indeed, there is more than a fleeting resemblance between the two figures. The *Ognissanti Madonna* looks out at the world impassively, an inscrutable giantess. Giotto's admirers have aptly likened her to a great abstract idol and an earth goddess. Yet she is also, in the words of the scholar Cesare Gnudi, "an eternal symbol containing all the grandeur of the medieval feeling for the transcendental and the divine."

At about the time that the *Ognissanti Madonna* was being put on display, Giotto may have been on his first and only venture beyond Italy's borders. Vasari asserts that he undertook commissions both at the new seat of the papacy in Avignon and elsewhere in France. That Giotto should have gone at least to Avignon seems logical: in exile no less than in Rome, the papacy prized the uses of art. However, no works remain in Avignon to prove Giotto's presence there. Of the "many very beautiful frescoes and pictures" referred to by Vasari, the only painting he singled out was one that he said Giotto brought home with him and later gave to his godson and star pupil, Taddeo Gaddi.

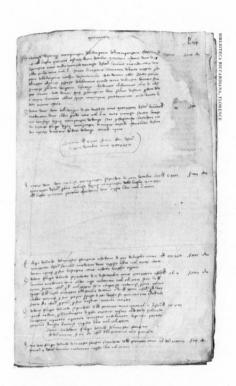

BIBLIOTECA RICCARDIANA, FLORENCE

Florentine bankers, many of whom were patrons of the arts, operated aggressively throughout Europe. This account book page records (in Old Italian) the advances paid by the Bruges and Paris offices of the Peruzzi family bank to a representative of Florence's powerful wool guild. The total of his expenses, for a wide-ranging business trip, is listed at top, opposite a notation that they included "eating, drinking, wages for his footmen, and the loss of two horses."

This work, according to Vasari, was a portrait of Clement V, the first pope to live at Avignon. Under Clement's successors the little town would blossom into a metropolis, with a magnificent papal palace and a papal court whose love of luxury would cause the poet Francesco Petrarca—Petrarch—who grew up in Avignon, to denounce it as the Babylon of the West. But all this lay in the future at the time of Giotto's presumed visit. Avignon was still in poor repute as a somewhat seedy haven for alchemists and sorcerers, and an air of impermanence clung to Clement and his retinue.

Although Clement gave occasional signs of wanting to take up the traditional papal residence in Rome, he lacked the will and the strength to defy his royal French mentor. His reign was unfortunate from first to last. It had begun on an ominous note at his coronation under King Philip IV's watchful eye at Lyons; during the papal procession, a shaky building wall fell in, knocking the tiara off the pope's head and throwing him off his horse. Thereafter he ailed chronically, taking to his bed for weeks at a time amid doctors and potions.

Little by little he surrendered the political power of the papacy so assiduously built up by his predecessors. He declared invalid—for France —the assertions by Boniface VIII of supremacy over temporal rulers. He stood aside when Philip, greedy for the wealth of the Knights Templars, the military order that had been a strong right arm of the Church in its crusades in the Holy Land, forced the Inquisition to try, torture and burn many of the Templars on the charge of heresy.

Clement's one big attempt to counter the King ended in bleak failure. When the throne of the Holy Roman Emperor fell vacant, Philip, seeking to extend his sway, coveted it for his brother Charles. Clement not only recognized the German electors' choice as emperor, Count Henry of Luxemburg, but encouraged him to go to Italy; he hoped thus to insure the protection of the papal lands and interests there. The new emperor, who took the title of Henry VII, was an idealist who truly believed that he could reconcile Italy's factions. Many of the dissidents welcomed him at first, and Dante hailed him as the heroic harbinger of national unity. Then, under pressure from Philip, Clement's support wavered and ceased. Henry's effort bogged down, and finally collapsed in his third year in Italy, when he died of malaria. He "who came to reform Italy before she was ready for it," as Dante mourned him, was buried in the Cathedral at Pisa. Clement died eight months later.

In the aftermath, Italians evinced a growing disenchantment with the papacy and an inclination to go it alone. The power vacuum produced by the failure both of pope and emperor was not hard to fill. In the south, the Angevin dynasty of King Robert of Naples, whom Henry had directly threatened, became further entrenched. In the north the major city-states became increasingly self-reliant. Since Robert depended on their bankers for loans, relations between north and south were usually amicable. More and more, money talked. The men who held the purse strings dominated all of civic life.

Most of these men were third-generation descendants of the founders of their family fortunes. They no longer had to venture forth as their grandfathers had done, drumming up trade at faraway fairs, traveling long distances at peril from pirates and highwaymen, defending their goods with their swords and fists. The family firms now had branches in London, Paris, Bruges and other key cities of Europe. Banking and commercial transactions could be supervised from a comfortable chair in the home office. And enough surplus capital had been amassed to afford fine town houses, country villas and leisure time to cultivate and patronize the arts and letters.

The shrewdness that had enriched the new magnate also guided his public behavior. Like today's tycoon, he cared about his image. The banker who endowed a handsome chapel in his family's name in some large and well-attended church knew that he stood to benefit. Common folk would find the chapel proof of his democratic ways, for it lay open even to the humblest churchgoer. Competitors would envy it as a mark of his prestige; clients would see it as a sign of the stability of his undertakings. An element of piety also figured in the donor's calculations. As the historian Wallace K. Ferguson observed, the affluent medieval Italian believed that money thus spent assured him of "credit both in this world and the next."

In Florence, sometime before 1320, such considerations moved two of the city's leading and rival banking families, the Bardi and the Peruzzi, to decide to build adjoining chapels in the great Franciscan church of Santa Croce. When it came to selecting a decorator, none but the best would do for Ridolfo de' Bardi and Giovanni Peruzzi, and both men turned inevitably to Giotto.

Giotto's murals in the Bardi and Peruzzi Chapels constitute, in Cesare Gnudi's phrase, "his last great message." He was to paint many more works after he finished at Santa Croce, but none of any major importance survives. The chapel walls themselves were for centuries hidden beneath layers of whitewash and overpaint and grime. Between 1958 and 1961, under the exquisitely tender ministrations of the restorer Leonetto Tintori, these layers were removed to reveal Giotto's original work. Many of the colors have faded and empty patches abound. The message, however, comes through. At the flood tide of his mature genius, Giotto summed up everything that he had mastered in art.

He summed up, moreover, with notable brevity. The Arena Chapel, which is itself the size of a small church, had given him much more room for maneuver. The Bardi and Peruzzi Chapels are high and narrow, each no more than about 14 feet wide and 17½ feet deep. Giotto's principal work in each chapel consisted of just six paintings, three on each side wall, one above another. The Bardi frescoes *(pages 144-145)* are scenes from the life of St. Francis, on the same themes used at Assisi. In the Peruzzi Chapel are three scenes from the life of St. John the Baptist and three from the life of St. John the Evangelist *(pages 146-147)*. Unexpectedly, Tintori's restoration disclosed that Giotto painted the Peruzzi scenes not in true fresco, but in tempera on dry plaster.

Although the scope afforded by the chapels was limited, Giotto manifestly found this no obstacle. Nowhere is there a sense of crowding or compression. Giotto worked with the ease and freedom that come only

BRITISH MUSEUM, LONDON

The top half of this manuscript illumination shows Italian bankers counting receipts; below, an eager crowd presses into one of their offices to borrow money. The Bardi and Peruzzi families of Florence established such successful banks in England that they were able to lend King Edward III enough capital to finance his war against France. But Edward could not raise the money to repay the loans, and by the mid-1340s the two Florentine houses were ruined.

with total self-assurance. Balanced arrangements, calm harmonies, figures and faces that are fully realized in their humanity—all these hallmarks of his past masterpieces recur. And there is much new besides. Occasionally Giotto employed the device of the multiple scene, linking several phases of one narrative within a single composition without cost to its unity or continuity. His architecture is more realistic than heretofore, providing a more logical and integrated spatial setting for his people. And throughout the chapels a greater refinement seems evident, perhaps inevitably for an artist of advancing years. There is less bulk to the figures, more grace of proportion; actions and emotions are muted.

These works clearly presage the classical dignity and gravity of Renaissance art. They show no lessening of Giotto's narrative and dramatic powers. Yet they are no longer folk tales but epics, no longer homely ballads but stately symphonies.

Santa Croce was to become the haunt of generations of budding artists, as much a magnet as the Louvre would be in a later age. While still apprentices, such future titans of the Renaissance as Donatello, Masaccio and Michelangelo would study Giotto's Bardi and Peruzzi murals, as well as his other works—since lost to view—in the chapels of the Giugni and the Tosinghi-Spinelli families.

More immediately, Santa Croce became a showcase for some of Giotto's more talented pupils, by now mature artists in their own right. Taddeo Gaddi decorated the Baroncelli family chapel with a series of frescoes of the life of the Virgin, and also painted a vast fresco, the *Tree of Life,* in the refectory of the church. For the Pulci family chapel, Bernardo Daddi painted scenes of the martyrdom of St. Lawrence and St. Stephen. For a second chapel endowed by the Bardi, Maso di Banco produced a series of five frescoes based on the legend of St. Sylvester and the Emperor Constantine.

As these men emerged from their anonymity as Giotto's assistants, one fact became plain: they would be neither routine imitators of the master nor flagrant rebels against him. They could not and did not hope to attain his heights. Franco Sacchetti's tales of Florence include an account of a convivial gathering of artists and the spirited discussion of who, next to Giotto, was the greatest painter of the time. No one disputed that Giotto should automatically be placed first, but the company could not agree on a candidate for second place. Among those present was Taddeo Gaddi; Giotto was not only his godfather but had been his employer for 24 years. Taddeo's reply to the question reflected the despair of those who follow in the wake of genius. Florentine art, he declared, was simply going downhill, and was dying a bit more as each day passed.

Taddeo's view was too pessimistic, as his own works and those of Maso and Bernardo prove. Although they lacked the simplicity and power of Giotto's art and the grandeur of his concepts, they displayed a high order of technical virtuosity. If they did not stir the heart and mind of the spectator, they arrested and gratified his eye. Long years in the shadow of a colossus had not stilled the urge for individual expression and experiment. Compared to Giotto's giant strides, the steps taken by Taddeo and Maso and Bernardo were tiny ones. But each in his own

MUSÉE CONDÉ, CHANTILLY

Direct evidence of the influence of Giotto and his contemporaries on later Northern European artists is provided by this early 15th Century manuscript illumination, which strongly resembles the fresco of the *Presentation of the Virgin* by Giotto's disciple Taddeo Gaddi (*page 150*). Designed as part of an inspirational calendar for the French Duc de Berry, the painting is by the Flemish brothers de Limbourg, at least one of whom had been to Italy and had studied the Florentine masters.

way helped propel the art of Italy directly toward its next great phase.

Of the three, the most original and imaginative was Maso. From what little is known of him, he seems to have been indifferent either to pursuing gain or placating patrons; at one point, he apparently failed to follow through on an order placed by the redoubtable Ridolfo de' Bardi himself, and Ridolfo retaliated by confiscating not only the uncompleted work, but Maso's paintbox, grindstone and other vital tools of his trade. Nevertheless, when Maso worked he left no doubt of his unusual gifts. His fresco of *St. Sylvester and the Dragon (pages 148-149)* is a triumph of stage design, wholly theatrical in its sharp contrast of lights and darks, its graphically delineated forms, its haunting architectural backdrop. Of all Maso's innovations, however, the most fruitful was his opening up of perspective; in this he clearly surpassed Giotto.

Taddeo, too, was intent on conquering space—"taking depth by storm," as the art historian Erwin Panofsky put it. Taddeo's attack on the problem differed from Maso's. He piled one solid structural form upon another, then placed them at oblique angles, perforce pulling the viewer's eye into the deepest recesses of the scene. His greatest success with this technique appeared in the Baroncelli Chapel fresco of the *Presentation of the Virgin (page 150)*, a painting that many later artists would try to emulate. Taddeo's huge fresco in the refectory of Santa Croce showing Christ on the Tree of the Cross from which all life stems *(pages 150-151)* was more ambitious in scope but of less moment to the mainstream of artistic advance. Like a tremendous tapestry, it teems with beautiful detail and complex imagery.

Bernardo's frescoes at Santa Croce proved only that he was less at ease with monumental paintings than with small-scale panels. He produced quantities of these portable works, usually depicting the Madonna and Child, for private devotional use *(page 148)*; one of his few commissions on public display was a painting on this theme for the dazzling marble tabernacle by the sculptor Andrea Orcagna for the church of Or San Michele *(page 185)*. Bernardo's preference for intimate size went hand in hand with a taste for delicate design, gentle lyricism and sparkling color. He thus served notice on his fellow Florentines that he had looked at the art of their ancient foes, the Sienese, and found it good. In Bernardo's works, the Sienese and Florentine styles of painting, hitherto so divergent, came together. An interplay began between the rival artistic ideas of the two cities, heralding a new chapter in Italian art.

In 1327 an event of great import for the painting fraternity took place in Florence. The *Medici e Speziali*—the powerful guild of the physicians and apothecaries—threw open its membership to experienced practitioners of art. The move was bound to enhance their standing in the community, and those who were sufficiently qualified took advantage of the invitation to join. Among them were Taddeo, Bernardo—and Giotto. Obviously Giotto needed no confirmation of his stature; moreover, a vainer man might have thought twice about putting himself on a par with his own pupils. Neither of these considerations seemed to trouble Giotto. He was entering his sixties and still immensely energetic. One last busy decade awaited him.

The Legacy and the Heirs

In the decades following Giotto's completion of the Arena Chapel at Padua *(pages 113-129),* the demand for his services took him to many other Italian cities, with the result that his hometown of Florence had scant opportunity to employ him. Nevertheless, two of Giotto's finest works during these years were executed for Florentine churches: the panel painting of the *Ognissanti Madonna (page 130),* and the frescoes for the chapels of the Bardi and Peruzzi families at Santa Croce.

Giotto was in his mid-fifties at the time of the Bardi and Peruzzi commissions, and his maturity is revealed in two important ways: the paintings contain a general note of measured calm, and almost every particular of his technique has been refined. While the Arena frescoes stir the emotions, the Santa Croce frescoes invite contemplation. Serenity, rather than urgency, is the keynote—and one that Renaissance masters were to adopt.

Close by the Bardi and Peruzzi Chapels are other chapels decorated by three of Giotto's disciples, Taddeo Gaddi, Maso di Banco and Bernardo Daddi. Long since taught by the master, and by now eminently qualified to pursue an independent course, Gaddi, Maso and Daddi were destined to take their places in the forefront of Florentine painting after Giotto's death. While they retained many of his principles, they devised their own distinctive styles, proving—as Giotto would have wished —that his heritage was a sturdy one.

Giotto's frescoes in the church of Santa Croce are in two small chapels to the right of the main altar, behind the candlelit Virgin in this photograph. The Bardi Chapel is nearest the altar; the Peruzzi Chapel adjoins the Bardi. The frescoes, which have withstood floods, retouching and even coats of whitewash, were only recently restored.

The Apparition at Arles, c. 1315–1320 (?)

The Trial by Fire, c. 1315–1320 (?)

For the Bardi Chapel, Giotto designed six scenes from the life of St. Francis, creating masterfully ordered figure groupings within complex spaces. For example, in *The Apparition at Arles (top)*, Francis appears as a vision to bless his followers, who are pictured in an intricately three-dimensional interior, set off by strong architectural forms that create a rhythm across the picture surface. In the frieze-like scene below, in which Francis miraculously demonstrates the power of his faith to a Moorish sultan, details such as the sweeping curves of the Muslim's robe *(right)* may have been inspired by the sinuous and expressive French Gothic style.

The Raising of Drusiana, mid-1320s (?)

The Dance of Salome, mid-1320s (?)

Giotto decorated the Peruzzi Chapel with scenes from the lives of St. John the Baptist and St. John the Evangelist. While the central figures, such as the Evangelist in the detail at left, were rendered in the simple, rugged style he used in Padua, his treatment of architecture within the scenes differs from that in the earlier work. In *The Raising of Drusiana (top)*, for example, a mighty fortress city looms above the monumental figures in the foreground, seeming to expand and deepen the space. The elaborate setting Giotto used for *The Dance of Salome (bottom)* is far different from the simple structures found in the Arena Chapel frescoes and shows the artist's increasingly sophisticated control over all the elements in his paintings.

GALLERIE NAZIONALE DI CAPODIMONTE, NAPLES

Bernardo Daddi: *Madonna and Child*, second quarter 14th Century

Maso di Banco: *St. Sylvester and the Dragon*, late 1330s(?)

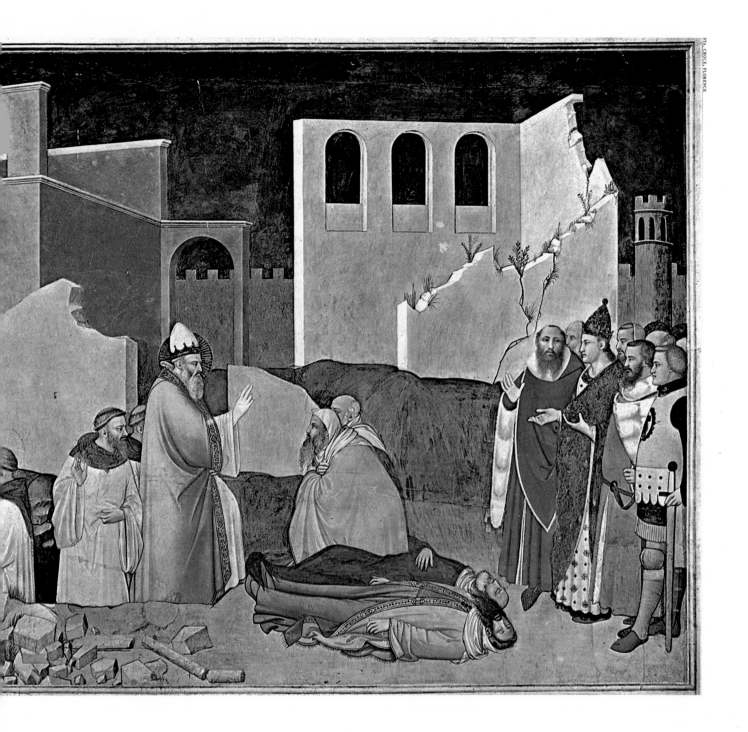

STA. CROCE, FLORENCE

Next to Giotto, his younger contemporary Bernardo Daddi seems to have been the most popular Florentine painter during the first half of the 14th Century. In answer to the growing demand for portable altarpieces for private worship, Daddi and his assistants produced small triptychs and single panels like the one at left, which is only 10 inches high. Daddi's work reflects the delicate, decorative quality of Sienese painting, but the bulk and solidity of his underlying forms are undeniably derived from Giotto.

Another of Giotto's followers, Maso di Banco, is known for his frescoes depicting the miracles of St. Sylvester.

While Maso's solid and expressive figures, like Daddi's, clearly reflect his debt to Giotto, his narrative technique is often more complex. In the painting above, for example, Maso integrates two separate episodes in a single scene. In a pit at left, St. Sylvester closes the mouth of a dragon who has killed two pagan elders; in the center the dead men are seen both prostrate and revived by the saint. Set amid ruins symbolizing the crumbling pagan world, the scene shows miracles that may have been enacted for the edification of the Emperor Constantine *(right),* whom the saint allegedly baptized.

BARONCELLI CHAPEL, STA. CROCE, FLORENCE

Taddeo Gaddi: *Presentation of the Virgin*, c. 1332–1338

REFECTORY, STA. CROCE, FLORENCE

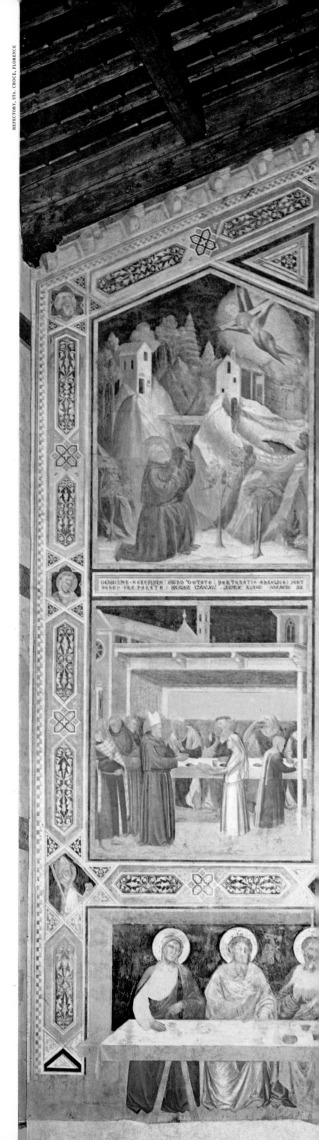

Like Daddi and Maso, Taddeo Gaddi, Giotto's godson and
assistant for 24 years, painted in the church of Santa Croce in Florence.
His frescoes of the Life of the Virgin in the Baroncelli Chapel
(located directly across the transept from the Bardi and Peruzzi
Chapels decorated by Giotto) mark his departure from his master's
conception of the use of architecture and space. The elaborate
perspective of his *Presentation of the Virgin (above),* with its many
levels and zigzagging steps, was a radical advance and one that
intrigued many later artists.

In the enormous fresco at right—which stands some 34 feet high
and occupies the entire end wall of the refectory at Santa Croce
—Gaddi flanked the mystical Tree of the Cross with incidents from
the lives of St. Benedict, St. Louis, St. Francis and Mary Magdalen.
At the base of the composition is Gaddi's version of the Last Supper.
This mixture of allegory, didactic painting and optical illusion—the
table in the Last Supper seems almost to project into the refectory
itself—has been called the most wide-ranging, complex and carefully
controlled fresco painted in the 14th Century.

Taddeo Gaddi: *Tree of Life,* c. 1340–1350

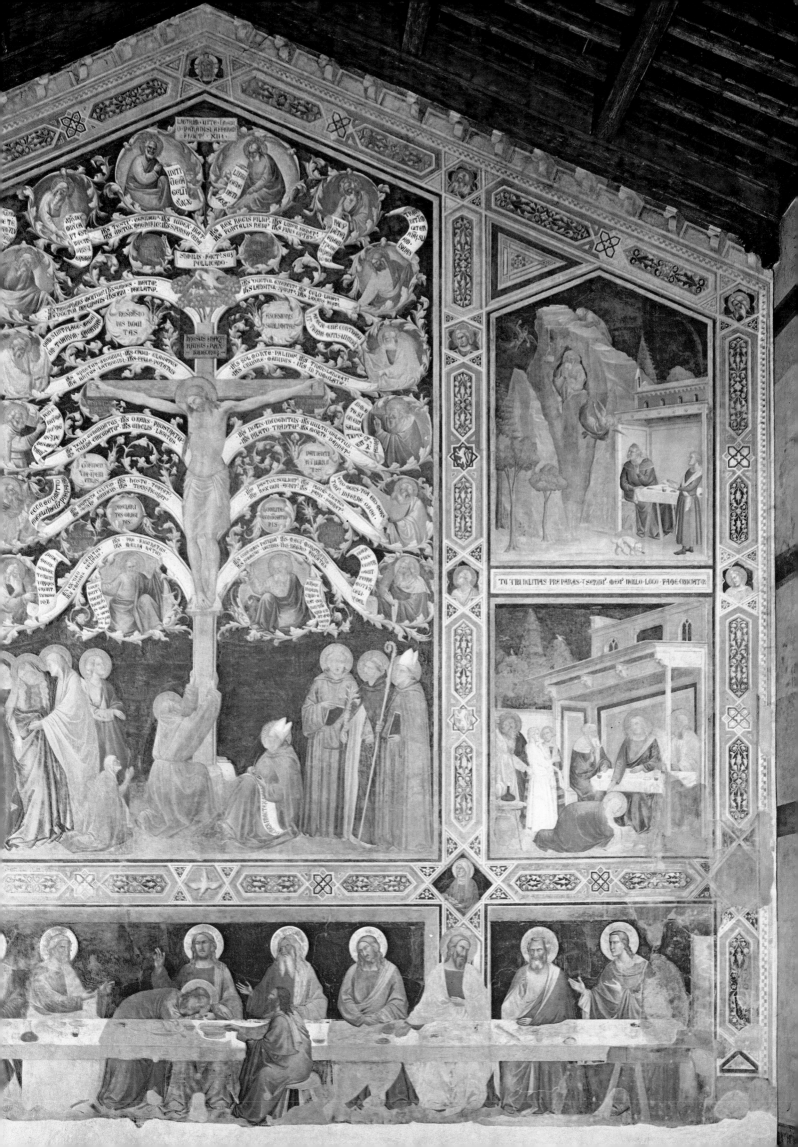

SECVRI TAS

SENÇA PAVRA OGNVOM FRANCO CAMINI·
ELAVORADO SEMINI CIASCVNO·
MENTRE CHE TAL COMVNO·
MANTERRA QVESTA DONA Ì SIGNORIA·
CHEL ALEVATA AREI OGNI BALIA·

VII

Giotto
the Architect

This detail from an allegorical fresco shows Security floating over peaceful farms near Siena. Her banner proclaims that all may walk and work freely because she has "removed all power from the guilty," a reference to Siena's effective city government, an oligarchy of nine wealthy men.

Ambrogio Lorenzetti:
The Effects of Good Government in the Country, 1337-1339, detail

In 1324, while Giotto was still at work on the Peruzzi Chapel frescoes, an Italian living in Paris produced a book that was to shatter the patterns of medieval thought. The author, Marsiglio of Padua, was a professor by calling and a gadfly by choice. His chief target was the papacy, and in attacking it he raised questions about the power of the Church that were to resound in the Reformation and far beyond. One pope denounced him as "the greatest heretic of the age." More effectively than any other man, Marsiglio gave voice to the rising secular spirit of his time, to the conviction that man's earthly welfare was no less urgent than his spiritual grace.

Marsiglio's treatise, a scrutiny of the relations of Church and state, declared that the people, not the papacy, were the real rulers of the Church; that the vast body of doctrine built up to fortify papal assertions of authority was a sham; that the laws of religion, with their emphasis on "truth" and "falsehood," should make way for reason; that everyone, even the unbeliever, should be free to follow his conscience.

The clergy, Marsiglio went on, should be restricted to such priestly functions as administering the sacraments, and the Church itself should be subordinate to the state, the highest authority of all. Marsiglio envisioned the ideal state much as Aristotle had described it more than 1,500 years earlier: as an institution created by the people, devoted to their welfare, and responsive to their will. While the state might be headed by a monarch and governed by an elite, neither was to have absolute authority; the people had the inherent right to approve the laws and, indeed, depose the monarch.

It was a measure of Marsiglio's courage—or cheek—that he could propound this last thesis and yet dedicate his book to a monarch: the new Holy Roman Emperor, Ludwig of Bavaria. Ludwig did not seem perturbed by the incongruity, or by Marsiglio's title in his honor, *Defensor Pacis*—defender of the peace—although he had just spent almost a decade at war with a rival for the throne. Politics even then made strange bedfellows, and Ludwig and Marsiglio found common cause in a common foe, Pope John XXII. Ludwig hated the Pope because John had encouraged the struggle for the throne in order to step in and arrogate imperial power to himself. Marsiglio's distaste, on the other hand, was less personal than philosophical.

The bracing intellectual climate of his own Padua—the same soil that had nurtured Giotto's outspoken astrologer friend, Pietro d'Abano —had shorn Marsiglio of any fear of opposing orthodoxy. At the time he wrote his book he was on the international faculty at the University of Paris, where he had met kindred spirits. The Frenchman Jean de Jandun encouraged him to prepare his treatise. The Englishman William of Ockham drew him into the thick of the dispute which, above all others, stirred the scholars' ire against Pope John. William, a Spiritual Franciscan, had renewed the demand that the Church revert to its absolute poverty of old. The Pope's academic supporters countered with the assertion that since Christ and the Apostles had fed the poor, they must have owned some property. After this hairsplitting performance came the worst blow: a papal pronouncement that those who urged a return to poverty were heretics.

Few events could have done more to alienate thinking men from the papacy and to insure an audience for Marsiglio's views. Many would have argued that it was unrealistic to expect the Church to divest itself of its immense wealth. Nevertheless, the pronouncement rankled, and the character of the current papal regime intensified the anger of the critics. For John XXII, born a shoemaker's son, was so adept at finance that he was called "Banker of the Holy See," and in the papal capital at Avignon austerity was a joke. The Pope slept on pillows edged with ermine, and wore cloth of gold from Damascus. In carpeted apartments hung with silks and tapestries he and his courtiers dined off table services of silver and gold. Staples of the cuisine included fresh-water fish shipped down the Rhone River in tanks, venison from the Alpine forests, strawberries and Beaune wine. To guard against poisoning, the wine was pre-tasted in special goblets adorned with serpents' tongues— supposed heralds of the truth.

For the liveries of his chefs, ushers and other servants, the Pope spent some 8,000 florins a year, and greater sums for rare furs and brocades for his relatives. His cardinals followed suit. Each had his own splendid residence and retinue. One cardinal required all or part of 51 houses for his followers; another required 10 stables for his horses. Still other prelates affected long hair, pointed shoes, and garments with checkerboard designs; some owned dogs and falcons, and employed jesters. All down the line ostentation of dress and manner prevailed.

One historian estimated that close to 20 per cent of the Pope's expenditures went for the upkeep and entertainment of his court, for dress, and for his kitchen and wine cellar. Despite lavish spending, however, outgo was more than matched by income. By the time John XXII died in 1334, the papal coffers were reported to contain currency, jewels and other treasures worth more than 25 million florins.

The legacy of his scholarly critics, however, was invaluable, and longer-lasting. It took the form of a torrent of words—written in Latin, translated into French, Italian and English, and read wherever men could read. Sheltered against papal wrath at the Emperor Ludwig's court at Munich, Marsiglio of Padua, Jean de Jandun and William of Ockham tirelessly turned out their tracts and broadsides. At the very least, their effect was to make people think about the role of the Church in their lives.

In the world of the artist, no overnight revolutions resulted. The Church continued to be his chief patron, and he continued to paint to its order. But a loosening of the bond began to be evident, both in the increased use of secular touches in religious paintings, and in a bolder interest in more purely secular paintings.

Signs of the trend appeared in Giotto's works in the final decade of his life. Some of his major commissions would scarcely have been conceivable in the artistic circles of his youth. At Castelnuovo, the residence of King Robert of Naples, he painted a fresco series of *uomini famosi*, famous men. In the palace of the despot of Milan, Azzo Visconti, he painted essentially the same theme under the title of *vanagloria*, worldly glory. Although both works are lost, it is believed that Giotto included such Biblical and Classical figures as Solomon, Samson, Hector, Paris, Achilles, Aeneas, Alexander and Caesar; he may also have depicted such feminine worthies as the Queen of Sheba, Helen of Troy, Dido and Cleopatra. Eventually this sort of gallery of the illustrious would become a standard feature of the painter's repertory. In Giotto's time, however, the theme was fresh. Celebrating not saints and martyrs but history's earliest heroes and heroines, it invited the viewer to take pride in the individualism of the human past, and to ponder its potential for the future.

A third commission set Giotto on still another new venture, this one for his own Florence. Heretofore the city's churches had monopolized his talents; he now undertook to decorate one of its civic buildings—the Palazzo del Podestà, headquarters of the city's top official. In the grand hall he painted a fresco extolling the virtues of Florence's republican government—the commune. According to a 16th Century description of the work, the commune was represented as a judge with a scepter in his hand and balanced scales over his head. The judge was assisted by four virtues: strength, prudence, justice and temperance. The writer found the work "a beautiful picture, of appropriate and ingenious invention." Unfortunately, only this brief word-picture remains; the fresco was destroyed.

Tradition has it that Giotto executed other frescoes for the Palazzo's chapel in which he relied on conventional religious subjects—scenes from the life of Mary Magdalen, and a *Last Judgment*—but with a notable difference in the latter work. Few artists who painted this theme portrayed the blessed and the damned in identifiable terms. Giotto produced an array of recognizable personalities from recent Florentine history, as Dante had done in his *Divine Comedy*. Appropriately, Dante—who had died in exile at Ravenna in 1321—was prominent among those whom Giotto memorialized in the Paradise section of his fresco. Under one arm Dante holds a book; in his right hand he clasps three pomegranates on a stem—symbolizing, one theory has it, the three realms of his masterwork, the *Inferno, Purgatorio* and *Paradiso*. Looking directly at Dante is a man believed to be Giotto himself.

The faces of Dante and Giotto may still be seen on the chapel wall. By now, however, their resemblance to the original portraits is conjectural. The Palazzo was later turned into a police headquarters and became known as the Bargello (the name it still bears) in honor of the captain of justice who ran it. The walls were whitewashed and the chapel was divided into two stories. A 19th Century decision to convert the building into a museum launched a flurry of restoration, in which —to the horror of art experts of the time—razors were used to remove the whitewash. Very little of Giotto's work remained unscathed, and a clumsy job of repainting completed the calamity.

In the traditional religious paintings that Giotto and his workshop continued to turn out for churches in Florence and elsewhere, hints of a new era in art are present although unproclaimed. The departure from the past is less a matter of overt change than of a subtle shift in psychological approach. The earlier intensity of expression is gone; an almost dispassionate calm prevails. It is as if the artist, while still revering the old familiar themes, were seeing them afresh in the serener light of reason. Like the Bardi and Peruzzi frescoes, these works show a classical restraint. The effect is the more impressive because most of the works that survive are small in scale; some were presumably once parts of larger altarpieces.

One of the survivors—the *Dormition of the Virgin*—has a triangular top suggesting that it may have been part of a gabled choir screen. It shows the Virgin's body being lowered into a sarcophagus; Christ stands above, holding His mother's departed soul in His hands. Around the bier are aged Apostles and youthful angels. Here Giotto has superbly arranged more than a score of figures in a limited space. The result is a measured drama in which each player has relevance. Michelangelo, Vasari wrote, was especially taken with the work, declaring that "it was not possible to represent this scene in a more realistic manner."

The last major paintings in which Giotto is believed to have provided the guiding hand are two large polyptychs that have remained intact: the *Coronation of the Virgin* for the chapel of the Baroncelli family at Santa Croce, and the *Virgin and Child Enthroned with Four Saints* for the church of Santa Maria degli Angeli in Bologna. Both works bear the inscription *Opus Magistri Jocti* (Work of Giotto the Master)—a token of his rise in reputation, since in his only other signed painting, at the Louvre, the inscription reads simply *Opus Jocti Florentini* (Work of Giotto the Florentine).

Giotto's actual participation in the polyptychs was probably limited to the design and to finishing touches, and his signature may simply have endorsed the efforts of his assistants. In any event, both works are manifest showpieces, intended to fill the eye rather than the heart. An unusual amount of decorative detail in the borders indicates that Giotto's pupils were straying from his fundamental concepts of simplicity and concentrated impact. The influence of Sienese art was making itself felt on his workshop, and apparently he did not object. At about the time of the Baroncelli and Bologna works, Giotto was personally engaged in a spectacular foray into the new fields of architecture and sculpture.

Giotto's loftiest patron in his last years was King Robert of Naples, grandson of the founder of the Angevin dynasty in Italy. At the time he called Giotto to his capital, Robert was ending the second decade of a 34-year reign. For a medieval monarch such longevity required luck as well as stamina, and the stars had favored Robert handsomely. He had staved off threats to his dominance in Italy from both the Emperor Henry VII and Henry's successor, Ludwig of Bavaria. He had the added advantage of amicable if wary relations with Pope John XXII; years earlier, in fact, the shoemaker's son had tutored the boy prince.

As Pope and King they had skillfully avoided a sticky situation over the question of Robert's right to his crown. The King's oldest brother had died, leaving a son; a second brother had joined the Franciscan order, eliminated himself from royal succession and subsequently died. Robert was crowned by the Pope in 1309 despite the claim of his nephew. In 1317 the Pope canonized the King's second brother as St. Louis of Toulouse. That year the celebrated Sienese painter Simone Martini visited the court at Naples and obligingly painted a scene of St. Louis conferring the crown on Robert. With the help of this work Robert argued, ex post facto, that the succession was his by "divine" right. Ordinarily, the papacy took a dim view of royal assertions of divine sanction, but Robert was useful as guardian of the papal interests in Italy, and John did not protest.

The same spirit of give-and-take marked Robert's relations with the Florentines. He depended heavily on the Bardi and the Peruzzi for loans; Florence, in turn, depended on him for protection against two belligerent local despots who successively harassed the city, Uguccione of Pisa and Castruccio of Lucca. Privately the Florentines loathed having to accept Robert as their *signore,* or virtual dictator, and having to quarter his troops in their midst; they were further mortified when Robert gave his protector's role to his son Charles, Duke of Calabria. But in 1328 Charles and Castruccio died within weeks of each other, suddenly freeing Florence of its double burden. With not even a tactful pause, the Florentines quickly restored their constitution and added even more democratic procedures for electing their officials.

It was in this somewhat strained atmosphere that Robert invited Giotto to Naples. Whatever annoyance the King may have felt toward Florence did not extend to its ranking painter, and Giotto, for his part, paid no heed to politics. Moreover, he had special assets to commend him to the King. During Charles of Calabria's one-and-a-half-year tenure in Florence, Giotto had painted his portrait in a fresco, showing him kneeling at the feet of the Virgin. And in the Bardi Chapel at Santa Croce, on the wall between the St. Francis frescoes, Giotto had produced a work even closer to the King's heart. The Bardi were eager to humor their royal debtor, and at their behest Giotto had painted four saints—one of them Robert's brother, St. Louis of Toulouse.

The King recorded his pleasure over Giotto's presence at his court in a public decree proclaiming that Giotto, "a painter familiar and faithful

GALLERIA NAZIONALE DI CAPODIMONTE, NAPLES

Art and statecraft are old companions. After Robert of Anjou became King of Naples, his proper place in the royal succession was questioned. To settle doubts and affirm his divine right to rule, Robert commissioned Simone Martini to paint the propagandistic picture above. It shows Robert kneeling before his brother, the former Bishop of Toulouse, who had been canonized as St. Louis. Louis receives the heavenly crown from two angels as he places the temporal crown on Robert's head.

This anonymous drawing is believed to record Giotto's original design for the multicolored marble bell tower of the Cathedral in Florence. Giotto supervised the construction of only the lowest stories before his death; the work was not finished for another 50 years.

to ourselves," was now a guest of the royal household, with all the honors and privileges of its other members. This was more than rhetoric; Giotto was given board and lodging at the palace, and a monthly salary.

He spent about four years in Naples, from 1329 to 1333—long enough to do a great deal of painting (and also long enough, records show, to engage in a local lawsuit, indicating that despite his latest good fortune he was still mindful of his money). As to his works at the palace and other buildings of the city, early references are vague. Besides his series of famous men, the only specific work mentioned is a series on the Old and New Testaments; according to Vasari, it included scenes from the Apocalypse based on ideas originally suggested to Giotto by Dante.

Anecdotes of Giotto's stay in Naples have proved more enduring than his paintings. Vasari recounted two that reveal, better than any record of payments or honors, how well Giotto stood with his august employer. Robert, Vasari declared, liked to chat with Giotto while he was at work, and on one blazing summer day remarked: "Giotto, if I were you, I would leave off painting for a while." Giotto quipped: "So would I—if I were you." Another time the King asked him to paint a miniature view of his kingdom. Giotto produced a picture of a donkey wearing one saddle and sniffing at another on the ground. Both saddles bore royal arms, crown and scepter. The baffled monarch asked for an explanation. The donkey, Giotto replied, represented Robert's subjects—and the fact that they were always seeking a change of master.

Another ruler might have found such impudence offensive, but Robert's affability toward men of arts and letters was one of the attractions that drew them to Naples. Giotto and Simone Martini were but two of many painters and sculptors brought in from Tuscany and from France. Other talents were also made welcome. During Giotto's sojourn the storyteller Boccaccio enjoyed the hospitality of the court; so later would Petrarch, Dante's successor as the literary titan of the time.

Neapolitan life was thoroughly congenial, but finally Giotto made his way back to Florence. Embarked on a new boom, his hometown had several ambitious building projects in prospect, and wanted to utilize his great gifts to the fullest.

On April 12, 1334, the Florentine government announced Giotto's appointment as *capomaestro*—chief master—of the building of the Cathedral, as well as chief of public works. The resolution it passed was a revelation of bursting pride:

"In order that the works which are being undertaken . . . may proceed in the most perfect manner, which is not possible unless an experienced and eminent man is chosen as leader in these works; and as in the whole world there is to be found none better qualified for that, and for much besides, than Master Giotto di Bondone . . . he shall therefore be named . . . as grand master and publicly regarded as such, so that he may have occasion to sojourn here for a long time; for by his presence many can have the advantage of his wisdom and learning, and the city shall gain no little glory because of him."

If there was a tinge of reproach in the implication that Giotto had been a hard man to nail down, his fellow Florentines were ready to make up for his protracted absences from home by piling on the work. He was charged with the supervision of the continuing building operations at the Cathedral, and with the construction and completion of the city's walls and fortifications.

Some of this work involved repairing damages wrought by a devastating flood that had struck the Arno Valley the preceding November. Not for more than six centuries—in November 1966—would the city again see such havoc. The rushing waters poured into Santa Croce and rose above the altar at the Baptistery. Parts of the city wall and the bridges spanning the Arno were swept away. Some believed that the disaster was a punishment for the luxuriance of the churches. Others sought no such supernatural explanation; indeed, with Giotto's help, work was begun on new building projects.

In an age of artistic versatility, the move from paintbrush to planning board could be achieved with a minimum of difficulty. So far as is known, Giotto's previous interest in architecture had expressed itself primarily in the skillful backgrounds of his frescoes. Yet so swiftly did he get down to his task that the first fruits emerged a little more than three months after his appointment. On July 18 the foundations were laid for the Cathedral's new bell tower; the Bishop of Florence blessed the first stone and a great public processional ensued.

Florence already boasted the 308-foot-high tower of the Palazzo della Signoria, designed by Arnolfo di Cambio three decades earlier; but it was a gloomy affair, and the ancient iron bell it housed, hoarsely calling citizens to assembly, had won it the derisive title of *La Vacca,* the cow. The Florentines' old foes, the Pisans, were finishing a tower that—despite an alarming tendency to lean even before its completion—was a marvel of tier upon tier of graceful arches and slender pillars. The Campanile of Florence would outshine Pisa's, if civic leaders had their way. Their resolution approving the project declared: "The Florentine republic, soaring even above the conception of the most competent judges, desires that the Campanile be built so as to exceed in magnificence, height and quality anything of the kind produced at the zenith of their greatness by the Greeks and Romans."

The hopes were met. The tower stands straight and sure on the city's skyline, a mating of delicacy and strength. Only the base was built by the time Giotto died, and the architect who finished the work, Francesco Talenti, modified the rest of Giotto's original plan. The influence of Giotto is more clearly seen in the little bas-reliefs designed to encircle the first story of the tower. There are 26 separate scenes. Together they unfold a panorama that begins with the creation of man, moves to scenes of his early nomadic life, and climaxes with his most advanced achievements. In all, the work is, as Eugenio Battisti has called it, "the most moving representation of the arts and sciences that European humanism ever produced." The new secular spirit of art was on the march.

Whether depicting man's first vintage in the scene of the drunken *Noah,* or his conquest of the air in the scene of *Daedalus,* these designs are masterpieces of swift statement. Yet they omit no pertinent details of nature or genre. A wonderfully realistic dog sits outside the tent of

The Campanile, which rises some 270 feet, shows that Giotto's successors took liberties with his plan. The treatment of windows and surface decoration differ markedly from the original scheme, and the building was topped with a cornice rather than a spire.

Jabal, the first herdsman; the scene called *Sculpture* contains the essential implements of that art, including a toolbox so finely wrought that even the keyhole of its lock is visible.

The task of translating the designs into marble fell chiefly to the sculptor Andrea Pisano. Andrea (no relation to the sculptors Nicola and Giovanni Pisano) had recently won fame for his 28 bronze reliefs on the doors of the Baptistery; a century later Lorenzo Ghiberti would fashion his *Gates of Paradise* for another side of this building. A stubborn tradition persists that Giotto himself carved several of the Campanile reliefs. Ghiberti asserted that he personally had seen clay models of these works, and that Giotto had executed the "first two" episodes, presumably the *Creation of Man* and the *Creation of Woman.*

Perhaps out of sentiment, another relief ascribed to Giotto is the scene of *Painting.* On the north side of the tower, it is one of a group including also *Sculpture, Grammar, Arithmetic and Geometry, Rhetoric, Logic* and *Harmony.* In *Painting,* the artist shown in his workshop has a worn look and a tired stoop to his shoulders; like Giotto, he is a man obviously in the sunset of life.

Sometime during Giotto's second year as *capomaestro,* the city allowed him to undertake a commission for the fearsome Lord of Milan, Azzo Visconti. Despite the Florentines' desire to keep Giotto busy at home, Azzo's request for his services was not to be taken lightly. One of Italy's most ruthless tyrants, he had killed his own uncle in pique at his growing power. Giotto went off to Milan to paint the *vanagloria* frescoes and presumably a number of other works.

Toward the end of 1336 Giotto came home for the last time. The new year was but eight days old when he died. The contemporary historian Giovanni Villani recorded that he was buried in the Cathedral "with great honors and at the expense of the commune." Legend has it that he was interred in the corner of the church nearest his beloved Campanile.

With Giotto's death, the leadership of Italian painting passed from Florence to Siena. In time it would be recaptured, but in the circumstances the change was predictable. None of the other Florentine artists could have tried to fill Giotto's shoes without feeling presumptuous; they had lived too long in his shade. Sienese painters, on the other hand, had steered their own course, and under auspices that were especially favorable to their art.

Long in the political orbit of Florence, Siena had channeled its energies into a conscious pursuit of the good life. In Sienese terms this meant material ease and above all elegance of surroundings. However inconsequential their little hill town might be in other matters, it would also be living testimony to their love for the beautiful. This wish was shared by one and all: from the widow who ordered a chalice for the Cathedral in her husband's memory, and the sausage makers who commissioned an altarpiece to their patron saint, to the ruling oligarchy of nine men who spared no expense on graceful fountains and plazas, splendid palaces and public buildings, and painting and sculpture to match. They beautified their town, the historian Ferdinand Schevill noted, "with that keen pleasure with which a lover adorns his mistress."

Giotto's bell tower is adorned with bas-reliefs representing a chronicle of human history from the Creation to his own day. One of them *(top)* shows a woman in a classical gown presiding over a loom, an appropriate Florentine subject. In another relief *(below)* an aged artist works intently over a panel painting while an untouched triptych awaits his attention. Many of the carvings, which were probably executed by others after designs by Giotto, were recently removed from the tower and replaced by copies in an effort to preserve the originals from deterioration.

MUSEO DELL'OPERA DEL DUOMO, FLORENCE

If self-interest was frequently involved, the Sienese did not mind. When the Palazzo Pubblico, the new city hall, was completed in 1309 and its sumptuous decoration begun, the populace fully endorsed the Council of Nine's declaration that it was "to the glory of the whole community that its rulers should enjoy surroundings which are fine, beautiful, and honorable." The palazzo's interior, the declaration emphasized, "should please the eye, bring joy to the heart, and satisfy everyone's senses." This was language even the humblest understood. It was also, inadvertently, a perfect summation of Sienese art.

Painters younger than Duccio were making more abundant use of ornamental detail and sinuous rhythms and rich colors in subtle juxtaposition. Some were also filtering the ideas of the Florentines, mastering three-dimensional form without the massive look, handling narrative not with urgency but with charm. The Sienese artist felicitously blended the mystic and the mundane. In a single painting he could impart both spiritual exaltation and a sensuous delight in costumes and settings. Sienese painters differed essentially from one another only in the vantage points from which they made their observations. Of Siena's three leading painters after Duccio, Simone Martini preferred the aristocratic view, the brothers Pietro and Ambrogio Lorenzetti the bourgeois view.

For the most part, the world Simone painted was a fairytale realm peopled by princesses and cavaliers and fastidiously free of discord. All is tasteful and genteel; he was obviously enchanted with the fast-vanishing chivalric ideals and courtly manners of the medieval nobility. His first known work—a huge fresco in 1315, covering a wall of the Palazzo Pubblico's main hall—was a *Maestà (page 165)*. Where Duccio four years earlier had made a solemn, hieratic display of this theme of the Virgin in majesty, Simone produced a lovely pageant. The Mother of Christ appears as a graceful queen, the saints and angels as lords and ladies-in-waiting; the canopy overhead resembles the tenting that shielded regal spectators as they sat watching a tourney of jousting knights.

Simone's flair for pomp and glitter attracted two illustrious patrons beyond Siena, King Robert of Naples and Cardinal Gentile da Montefiore, one of the custodians of the papal funds. At Naples Simone portrayed Robert's brother, St. Louis of Toulouse, in robes as elaborate as any earthly king could wish. For the Cardinal he painted an entire small chapel at the Basilica of St. Francis in Assisi with a superb series of frescoes of the life of the early missionary bishop St. Martin of Tours.

The fact that Martin had lived long before the concept of chivalry arose did not deter Simone; he even depicted the knighting of the saint *(pages 166-167)*, down to such traditional detail as the affixing of his spurs. Simone's imagination knew few bounds. Back in Siena, he painted an *Annunciation* as no other artist had envisioned it; the angel Gabriel appears as a handsome blond chevalier in costly brocade, while the Virgin, a slender patrician whom he has surprised at her reading, recoils at this intrusion into her chamber.

One of the few purely secular works of Simone's that survive, a portrait of the professional soldier Guidoriccio da Fogliano *(pages 168-169)*, gave the painter an opportunity to anchor his illusions to a contemporary event. Depicting Guidoriccio's recent victorious defense of Sienese territory, Simone revealed a sharp eye for detail in the warrior's features and garb and in the countryside around his native city. But he chose to temper this realism by abstracting the landscape and withholding all other figures from it. In the end, Guidoriccio remains a solitary giant against the sky—a fitting creature of Simone's romantic reveries.

The visions of Pietro and Ambrogio Lorenzetti were more prosaic. They shared all of Simone's delight in color and ornament and the comfortable minutiae of life, but none of his nostalgia for the customs and glories of a dwindling upper class. It was Siena's middle class that concerned the Lorenzetti, and it was the quality of these solid citizens that they celebrated in their art.

Pietro and Ambrogio were frankly receptive to artistic ideas from Florence. When Simone borrowed, it was largely from the French Gothic, a style attuned to his own innate lyric grace. Florentine painting, bold and insistently dramatic, may well have struck him as vulgar. The Lorenzetti, without denying their elegant Sienese heritage, saw that they could profitably infuse it with Florentine vigor and clarity.

Ambrogio, in fact, lived in Florence for a number of years; he was even admitted to membership in the guild in the same year as Giotto. Whether he knew Giotto is not recorded, but he can hardly have missed the evidences of his genius. So far as is known, Pietro never joined his brother in Florence. Possibly his opportunity to learn from its painters may have come at the basilica at Assisi, where he executed three scenes in a series of powerfully expressive frescoes of the Passion in the south transept of the lower church.

In all, more than two dozen works of the Lorenzetti survive. For some four decades of painting activity, the number presumably represents only a fraction of their actual achievement. But what remains is enough to prove the brilliance of their merger of the two seemingly irreconcilable styles of Siena and Florence. To this feat, moreover, the Lorenzetti added their own innovations—in the depiction of convincing interior spaces, in the creation of figures that are warm and lifelike, and in landscape rendering.

Pietro's masterpiece is his triptych of the *Birth of the Virgin (pages 170-171)*. The scene, an interior, bears the authentic marks of a well-appointed bourgeois home; the tiled floor, the gaily adorned chest, the checkered coverlet on the bed, all reaffirm the Sienese joy in design and in material objects. Yet the people portrayed are as weighty and down-to-earth as Giotto's; the two neighbors chatting as they bring gifts for the newborn Mary are genre at its best. Pietro's major stroke, however, was the faultless illusionism of his painted framework, and its use both to convey an impression of the depth of the room and to carry over the action from one segment of the scene to the next. For the first time, a painting presented an interior that was a logical entity in itself, fully open to the viewer's gaze and understanding.

Ambrogio's masterpiece, a colossal sequence of frescoes on the subject of government covering three walls of the Sala della Pace at the Palazzo Pubblico, is both secular and propagandistic. The hands are the hands

BIBLIOTHÈQUE NATIONALE, PARIS

Avignon's lively and worldly papal court supported a number of artists, among them the great lyric poet Petrarch, who served as a household chaplain for an Italian cardinal. This sketch, the only authenticated portrait of the writer, was made by Lombardo della Seta, a disciple, secretary and friend who later completed Petrarch's unfinished poems.

of Ambrogio, but the voice is the voice of Siena's oligarchy, at once reminding its citizens that things had never been better for them, and that they might do a lot worse. It is an astonishingly ambitious panorama *(pages 172 through 175),* in which Ambrogio produced a documentary of 14th Century life that has proved to be invaluable source material for historians. The backdrop of one section depicting the effects of good government is Siena itself; in the foreground its people go about their tasks and pleasures. What might have evolved into a jumbled tapestry emerges as a topographical and structural triumph. Ambrogio capped his effort with a glimpse of the countryside beyond Siena that is the first truly convincing landscape in Italian art.

In 1340, a year after Ambrogio completed his great opus, Simone Martini journeyed to Avignon at the bidding of Pope Benedict XII. Like his predecessor John XXII, Benedict valued the uses of display. John had begun to expand the old episcopal residence that was the core of the papal palace. Benedict was continuing the project, building five massive towers that added the look of a fortress. The huge white structure on the rocky heights of Avignon was, indeed, designed as an impregnable citadel. Its walls were 13 feet thick and almost windowless; by one means or another, the darkness within had to be offset.

The Pope commissioned Simone to decorate two chapels in the palace, and the hall of the consistory. Whether his gay colors did much to lighten the gloom can only be surmised; the frescoes are gone. Time has been almost as unkind to other frescoes he painted at the Pope's behest in the Cathedral of Notre Dame des Doms. All that remains are the eroded fragments of several scenes.

Nevertheless, Simone's stay at Avignon was destined to be remarkably fruitful. The free-spending papal court was beginning to draw artists from Northern France and Flanders, from Bohemia and Catalonia. Some had worked as manuscript illuminators for princely patrons with a passion for miniature design. In the exquisite style of the renowned painter from Siena they recognized a kinship of tastes. They found a special appeal in a number of small, jewel-like panels that Simone executed as parts of larger works. Six have been preserved: an *Annunciation,* scenes from the Passion of Christ, and a *Return of the Saviour from the Temple.*

Simone made another admirer—and friend—in Petrarch, now back from his travels. For the poet Simone produced two miniatures. One, for the frontispiece of a manuscript of Virgil, shows the old Roman seeking inspiration in a forest. The other was a portrait on parchment, now lost, of Petrarch's beloved Laura. Petrarch responded in a grateful sonnet which included these lines: "Certainly my Simone must have been in Paradise / of which this lady forms a part / There he saw her and portrayed her on paper / to give evidence here below of her beautiful face. . . ."

Some years later Petrarch would pass his judgment on both Giotto and Simone. Along with his treasured memento of Laura, he owned a Madonna by Giotto, which he bequeathed to his mentor, the Lord of Padua. In a letter to a friend he reminisced: "I have known two painters, talented both, and excellent: Giotto of Florence, whose fame amongst the moderns is great, and Simone of Siena."

BIBLIOTHÈQUE NATIONALE, PARIS

Partly to escape the ugly, overcrowded city —and also to remove himself from the presence of a married woman with whom he had fallen in love—Petrarch retreated in 1337 from Avignon to Vaucluse, a lovely mountain village. His sketch, in the margin of a book, shows a church, a fishing heron and a local cave that is the source of the River Sorgue. It bears the poet's Latin inscription, "Solitude beyond the Alps, my greatest joy."

The Sienese Flowering

Siena had long lived in the shadow of Florence, a wealthier, more powerful rival, but by the opening years of the 14th Century it had attained a political stability and an economic prosperity of its own, marked by an increasingly fierce civic pride. A traditional love of beauty and worldly possessions, combined with a strong religious fervor, pervaded all levels of Sienese society. Commissions for art, long bestowed almost exclusively by the Church, began to come from civic groups, guilds and wealthy individuals. With this secularization of patronage came a change in the subject matter of paintings, and even in the treatment of religious themes. Siena began to see itself reflected in its art in a totally new way.

During those years of affluence three outstanding Sienese painters helped to satisfy the public demand with a wide variety of works. Simone Martini painted a sumptuous *Maestà (right)* and a heroic military portrait of a Sienese general at the behest of the town council for one of its meeting halls. Simone's great contemporary, Ambrogio Lorenzetti, painted for the Palazzo Pubblico a magnificent series of frescoes on the subject of government, a particularly vital concern of the freedom-loving Sienese. Ambrogio's older brother, Pietro, brought many colorful and beguiling scenes from everyday life into his religious works. Together, these artists presented to their fellow citizens, and to posterity, a vivid picture of a proud and prosperous medieval town.

To celebrate Siena's enlightened government, its council commissioned a richly figured *Maestà* for the council chamber. It presents the Virgin—to whom the city was dedicated—as a medieval queen enthroned beneath a royal canopy; in an inscription on the painting, she promises to answer the prayers of the just—but to be harsh on oppressors of the weak.

Simone Martini: *Maestà*, 1315.

LOWER CHURCH OF S. FRANCESCO, ASSISI

Simone Martini: *Investiture of St. Martin*, 1324–1328, detail at right

Soon after the unveiling of his *Maestà*, Simone Martini became so famous that he was offered 50 ounces of gold annually to paint at the court of Robert of Anjou, King of Naples. While there, Simone felt at home amid the pageantry and color of court life, with its noble knights, lovely ladies and strolling troubadours. Increasingly, these elements crept into even his religious pictures, as they had to a lesser degree in his *Maestà*.

One such work, painted a few years later, is the fresco above, part of a series Simone was commissioned to paint in a chapel of the lower church at Assisi. The narrative was the traditional story of the Fourth Century converted pagan soldier who became St. Martin, but Simone transformed it into a glorification of medieval chivalry. Here, amid grooms, pages and musicians (seen in the detail at right), St. Martin is being made a knight by the Emperor Constantius in a gay and colorful ceremony. It was a rite whose form and trappings Simone knew well —he himself had been knighted for his work some years earlier by a grateful King Robert.

· ANO · DÑI · M · CCC · XX · VIII ·

PALAZZO PUBBLICO, SIENA

Simone Martini: *Guidoriccio da Fogliano,* 1328, detail at left

By 1328 aggressive marauding Pisans had seized control of Siena's
neighboring towns of Montemassi and Sassoforte. The Sienese thereupon sent
a general, Guidoriccio da Fogliano, to retake them. When Guidoriccio was
successful, the joyous town council of Siena commissioned Simone to immortalize
the soldier's feat in an equestrian portrait.

In the Palazzo Pubblico, directly opposite his peaceful *Maestà,* Simone
painted a vast martial tableau, almost 11 feet high and 32 feet long. It shows the
stout warrior astride his magnificently caparisoned horse, riding out from his
tented camp *(far right)* past the captured city of Sassoforte, from whose battlements
his banners already fly, on his way to besiege Montemassi. Behind Guidoriccio,
who rides along the bottom of the picture as if through space, is the bleak
landscape outside Siena, clearly recognizable but unusually stark and empty. The
artist has suppressed all irrelevant details and reduced the elements to simplicity
—no human figure other than Guidoriccio's can be seen—to concentrate all
attention on the purposeful and silent rider.

MUSEO DELL' OPERA DEL DUOMO, SIENA

Little is known of the youth of Pietro Lorenzetti, but some time after his apprenticeship—which he may have served with the earlier Sienese master Duccio—he went to work in Assisi, where the fresco cycle of the life of St. Francis, possibly done by Giotto, made a deep impression on him. In any case, Pietro was evidently familiar with Giotto's work, and he seems to have sought to build into his own art a similar sense of the monumental and a feeling for emotion. However, Lorenzetti's painting is truly Sienese, full of charming detail and luxurious color.

Among Pietro's most inventive works is this triptych of the birth of the Virgin. It is an important landmark in the history of art: the first true interior scene ever painted. In most previous portrayals of a room the whole house was shown (as, for example, in Giotto's depiction of the birth of the Virgin on page 117). Pietro, however, showed only the interior, and he united the panels by carrying elements of the scene from one to another: for example, the figure of the woman sitting and holding a fan before the Virgin's mother, Anna, appears partly in the right-hand panel as well as the center one. The frame is incorporated into the rooms as part of their architecture, and forms a logical extension of the interior space. The tiled floor, the vaulted ceiling and even the blanket pattern serve to unify the space and give it perspective and depth. Pietro added another spatial device in the left-hand panel, in which Joachim anxiously awaits news of the birth. In the background is an open window facing a courtyard. The viewer's eye is drawn back into that area in such a way that the three-dimensional aspect of the interior seems to be further confirmed.

Finally, Pietro's triptych resembles life as it might have been lived in Siena. The figures are not distant, otherworldly creatures but townspeople with a pride in their home and its comforts. Pietro has brought a holy event down to earth.

Pietro Lorenzetti: *Birth of the Virgin*, 1335-1342

VOLGIETE GLIOCCHI A RIMIRAR COSTEI VOI CHE REGGIETE CHE QVI FIGVRATA 7 PSVE CELLECA CORONATA LAQVA

Ambrogio Lorenzetti, Pietro's younger brother, was a philosopher, a cosmographer and a brilliant map maker as well as a talented painter. He put many of his skills to use in painting cityscapes and landscapes of dazzling beauty and perceptive observation. The vast scene shown here, some 13 feet high and 27 feet long, is part of a fresco cycle in Siena's Palazzo Pubblico depicting the effects of good and bad government in the city and the country. The scenes are framed within a decorative border inset with medallions representing the arts, the planets and the seasons. This section of the fresco shows the city bustling with trade, merry fun and useful work

Ambrogio Lorenzetti: *Good Government in the City*, 1337-1339

—a solid endorsement of Siena's council of wealthy merchants. Glimpsed at the far right is a scene of rural well-being which appears in greater detail on page 152.

Ambrogio depicted his city with a keen eye for detail. Many of the buildings are similar to still-standing Sienese structures—including the Cathedral, which the workmen at top center are presumed to be erecting. In the streets below, Tuscan donkeys bear their grain sacks and a sheep drover moves his flock; in the center a class is in full session in an arcade, while maidens clad in fashionable silks dance to a tambourine and a lady with her entourage rides off to the left. All is in order in Siena.

Overleaf: Detail of girls' dance from *Good Government in the City*

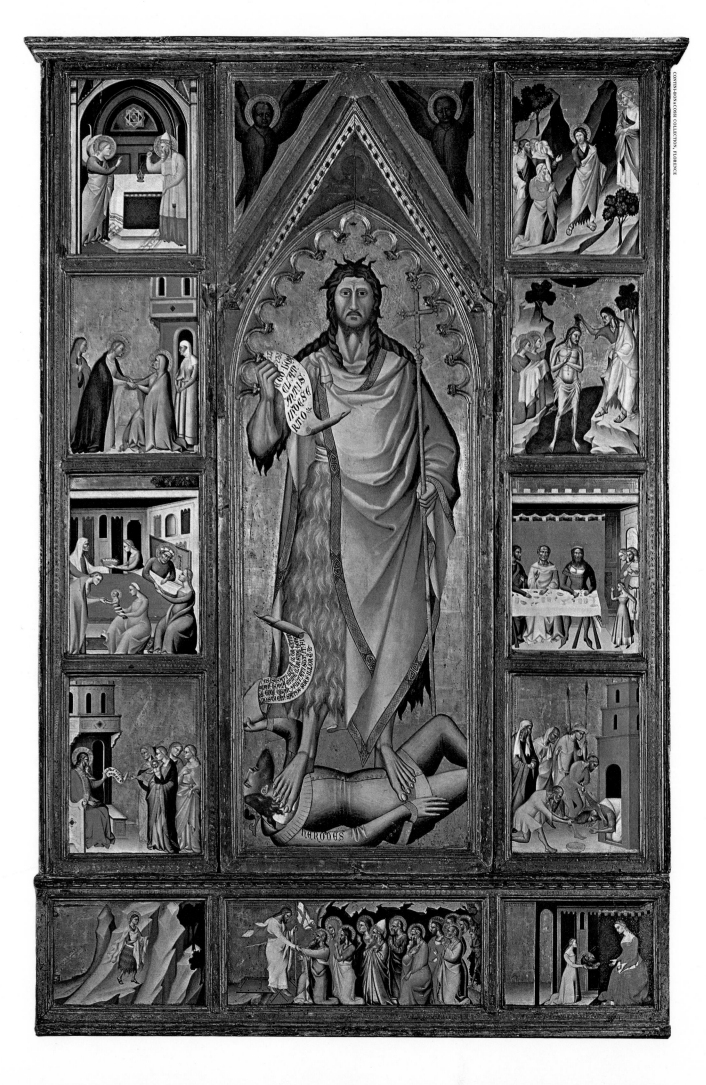

CONTINI-BONACOSSI COLLECTION, FLORENCE

VIII

A Time
of Affliction

Painting in mid-14th Century Tuscany reflected the stern morality of a people whose lives had been shattered by decades of political unrest, famine and many epidemics of plague. Reverting to both the mood and format of earlier works, this altarpiece shows a gaunt and austere John the Baptist, surrounded by scenes from his life and trampling with clawlike feet upon a figure of King Herod, who had ordered the saint's beheading.

Giovanni del Biondo: *Altarpiece of the Baptist,* third quarter of the 14th Century

At the time of Giotto's death in 1337, Florence was a city in sight of a golden age. Education and social services flourished along with art and architecture. Of a population of 90,000—double that of Giotto's youth—11,000 were boys and girls who were enrolled at schools, learning to read and write, wrestling with grammar and logic, training in the vocational use of the abacus and Arabic numbers. Thirty hospitals stood ready to minister to the indigent sick. Prosperity was high. Some 200 textile firms employed fully a third of all Florentines. Eighty banks thrived on an influx of deposits. The commune itself reaped a revenue of 300,000 golden florins, more than some kings could boast.

The compiler of these statistics was the same Giovanni Villani who had meticulously recorded Giotto's burial at public expense. Villani gloried in facts and figures, and if some of his findings proved less rosy than his patriotic heart might have wished, he nevertheless reported them in his *History of Florence.* While 6,000 Florentines "had the most luxurious and splendid dwellings," 17,000 others were beggars and 4,000 were sheer paupers. While the people had their choice of 110 churches to attend, they also drank so much that the tax on wine sales accounted for one fifth of the city's income; their surly manners necessitated another tax on fist fights. While the civic budget made room for salaries for festive trumpeters and kettledrummers, it also supported such killjoys as spies and one official whose sole duty was to guard against excesses of female fashion. The low-cut bodice provoked special concern, but despite its denunciation as a "window of hell" it continued to be a badge of womanly defiance.

On occasion Villani looked heavenward. In 1337, he noted, two comets appeared in the sky within a short time of each other. Like many medieval men of intellect, Villani stoutly believed in celestial portents. "Whatever they may be," he wrote, "every comet is the sign of some event in the world, and generally a malignant one. . . . Wheresoever the comet extends its mastery, it produces many evils, such as famine, pestilence, revolution, and other grave occurrences."

Villani penned this passage in the light of hindsight; he failed to mention whether the comets had filled him with foreboding at the time they appeared. It would have been hard for any Florentine to believe, in 1337, that in a few short years his comfortable world would begin to crumble; that a full decade of crisis and calamity awaited him; that a disaster of untold dimensions would befall Florence and all Europe, changing the 14th Century's outlook and art and way of life.

The first severe blow was dealt Florence from far-off England. King Edward III blithely repudiated huge unpaid portions of loans totaling 1,365,000 florins that had been furnished him by the Bardi and Peruzzi, and had helped launch what was to become the Hundred Years War with France. Edward was in constant straits; he once even pawned the crown jewels. Still, the two great Florentine banking houses had adjudged him a risk worth backing. They hoped to gain, among other handsome favors, a monopoly of England's export trade in wool.

The magnitude of Edward's default touched off a cataclysmic chain reaction. The London branches of the Bardi and Peruzzi went under immediately. King Philip VI of France, incensed at the Italians' financing of his foe across the Channel, seized their French companies. In Florence, panic produced a run on every bank in the city. On its heels came a new shocker: the Florentine government stopped repaying the large debt it had incurred in small sums from its citizens for a protracted and fruitless campaign—in competition with Pisa—to conquer the coveted city of Lucca.

In the mounting crisis the Bardi and Peruzzi, along with other nobles and rich merchants, saw a potential savior in the curious person of a French adventurer, Walter of Brienne, titular Duke of Athens. The Duke not only had redoubtable military skill, but was the husband of a niece of King Robert of Naples. Through this link the Bardi and Peruzzi hoped to placate Neapolitan creditors who were calling in their deposits and threatening the two banks' final ruin. Under the excuse of civic emergency, the Florentine commune made way in 1342 for the Duke's despotic rule. But he proved an ineffectual leader and a year later he was driven from the city. His worst offense, from the magnates' standpoint, was that he had given a voice in his regime to the lesser guilds—the petty shopkeepers and artisans—and had even shown favor to the *ciompi*, the proletariat. These acts would haunt the Florentine power structure for decades.

By January 1345 the parent banks of both the Bardi and Peruzzi had collapsed. Other banks and businesses sank with them. Little people who had placed their funds with the Bardi and Peruzzi faced destitution. Trade began to fall off sharply. "When these two pillars of business failed," Villani wrote, "every other merchant was distrusted and believed dishonest." For someone so matter-of-fact, Villani had an unexpected explanation of events. "Everything happens," he concluded, "because of the fallible fortune of temporal things in this miserable world." Countless other Italians—and Europeans—were to take up this tone of somber introspection as sorrow piled upon sorrow.

One large new grief visited upon Tuscany was the ravaging of its countryside by foreign mercenaries. In recent decades Florence and other cities had taken to importing soldiers of fortune—Germans, English, French and Hungarians—to stand in for local townsmen in Italy's perennial wars. These hirelings now began to realize that they could divert themselves profitably between paid engagements. In organized bands they roamed the hills and valleys plundering, raping and killing. The boldest freebooter of all was Werner von Urslingen, whose breastplate bore the inscription *Enemy of God, of Pity, and of Mercy*. While the Florentines were in the throes of their internal troubles with the Duke of Athens in 1342 and 1343, Werner made a clean sweep of Tuscany, finally heading home across the Alps with a huge haul of ill-gotten gains including 2,500 florins given him by Siena simply to go away.

There was another kind of incursion that Florence had to endure along with the rest of Europe: the onset of a new horde of papal tax collectors. Clement VI, who took office in 1342, sounded the theme of his regime with the remark that his predecessors had not known how to be popes. The opulence of Avignon under Clement required a further systematizing of the papal finances, and Clement rose to the challenge.

Traditionally, a major portion of papal revenues came from fees and taxes levied upon prelates directly appointed by a pope. Whoever secured a benefice this way paid, among numerous other charges, a fee at the time of his appointment and a tax after his first year's incumbency —amounting to about half the revenues from the benefice for that year. He also assumed any debts owed the papacy by previous incumbents. To offset these obligations he was allowed to impose a variety of charges on his own appointees, men below him in the hierarchy.

The Avignon popes had begun to add to the number of appointments made from the top. Clement's accomplishment was to expand this practice to the point where almost the only benefice left to be filled locally was the parish priesthood. Since all papal appointees were required to pay their fees and taxes directly to the papal treasury, the bonanza for Avignon was obvious. Moreover, Clement openly invited applications—for a fee—for future vacancies in benefices; an estimated 100,000 hopeful clerics responded. One caustic critic had the temerity to invade the Pope's presence with a donkey wearing a petition for a bishopric around its neck.

Europe was methodically organized into seven tax-collecting areas, but the agents assigned to the task found it a perilous one. Many were beaten, jailed, strangled or drowned. Prelates stripped of their appointive power and sources of revenue shared their resentment with laymen at every level. Edward III of England, although hardly qualified to cast any stones, reminded the Pope that "the successor of the Apostles was commissioned to lead the Lord's sheep to the pasture, not fleece them." The average citizen's reaction was in the end more devastating. Sometimes he witnessed a papal collector's public excoriation of his bishop for tax delinquency. Sometimes he saw his pastor reduced to penury, and religious services curtailed. Inevitably such incidents colored his view of Church authority, and increasingly he turned away.

Florence was hit by natural as well as man-made havoc. Virtually every family lost a relative in a pestilence in 1340. The failure of the

Tuscan harvest caused a famine in 1346. Violent hailstorms damaged the next crop and created new food shortages in 1347. Such phenomena were periodic recurrences in Florentine life, but this time recovery was destined to be delayed by the advent of a disaster more horrible than the wildest imagination could have foretold: the Black Death of 1348.

This evil, which has since been diagnosed as a type of bubonic plague, caused its victims to spew up blood and develop lumps on their bodies the size of eggs; death came in one to three days. The plague was Asian in origin. Mongol besiegers brought it to the walls of a Genoese trading station at Kaffa on the Black Sea, and rats carried it aboard Genoese galleys bound for Constantinople, Genoa, Pisa and Marseilles. Wherever these vessels put in, epidemics broke out. The ships were driven off with fiery arrows and missiles, and drifted ghostlike at sea; but the damage was done.

The techniques of medieval mural painters have often been revealed during efforts to preserve their work. The details above are from *The Triumph of Death*, a fresco attributed to Francesco Traini *(page 188)*. After the work was badly damaged by fire during World War II, restorers removed sections of the painted outer layer of plaster *(lower picture)*. Beneath it, on the rough inner plaster, they found remarkably complete sketches *(top)*, which had evidently served as a guide for the artist. Such drawings are called "sinopias," after the ancient city of Sinope, where the red earth pigments originally used for the purpose were found.

CAMPOSANTO, PISA

The plague struck Florence in April 1348. It swept the rest of Italy and France the same year, Britain in 1349, and Scandinavia and Germany in 1350. Among those who perished were the chronicler Villani, William of Ockham, Petrarch's Laura, the brothers Lorenzetti, and Giotto's pupil Bernardo Daddi. The Florentine population was halved. The final toll throughout Europe was about one third of its inhabitants.

Eyewitness accounts reveal the same grisly pattern from city to city. Fear of contagion drove parents from children and wives from husbands. The luckless lay attended, if at all, by dullards unaware of the danger. Burials were hasty and often in common pits. The unscathed reacted according to their lights. Some sought isolation; Pope Clement VI, refusing all visitors, secluded himself in his chamber, where huge fires roared constantly in the hearth, presumably as a repellant. Other people left the cities for the relatively healthful countryside. Others stayed behind. Some Florentines embarked on one long carouse, "straying by night and day from tavern to tavern," Boccaccio reported, "drinking beyond measure and limit."

For Boccaccio, the plague provided the basis of his celebrated *Decameron,* which describes how seven young ladies and three young bloods fled Florence for the safety of a villa in the hills. There they gave themselves up to pleasure, entertaining each other with gay and often salacious stories and observing the rule that none would bring in from outside "any news other than joyous."

In the aftermath of the plague, homes stood empty and fields untilled. Schools and universities closed for lack of teachers and pupils, churches and charitable services for lack of priests and monks. Surviving institutions had to hobble along with untrained personnel. Courts had to cope with vast tangles over property ownership and inheritance. The crafts were crippled by the loss of masters who could pass their skills on to journeymen and apprentices.

Social and economic dislocations were innumerable. Some noble lines died out entirely. On the whole, the rich came through relatively unharmed; the Bardi and Peruzzi hung on to their personal wealth. But they had to make room for others shrewdly building on the ruins, including members of an obscure clan named Medici. The irrepressible trading instincts of the Florentines soon spawned a new set of entrepreneurs, some of whom had turned a tidy profit from the sale of drugs and shrouds. The plague had also perversely favored the survivors among the laboring classes. With their ranks thinned out, they could pick and choose among employers, and demand higher pay; the stable boys and servant girls of Florence asked for a minimum wage of 12 florins a year, and manual laborers insisted upon three times their normal previous wage. Laws compelling work at pre-plague rates curbed such effrontery —and sowed the seeds of later proletarian revolt.

Spiritually, almost every individual was restive. Already disenchanted with Avignon, people increasingly tended to keep their own moral counsel. Riotous living was one result. Giovanni Villani's brother Matteo, inheriting the historian's mantle, reported that those who indulged in "delicate viands . . . games of chance . . . unbridled lechery . . . indecent manners in their garments" did so because "now they thought that God's hand was unstrung."

While some people abandoned all faith and formed cults of Satan, others became religious hysterics. New recruits flocked to the sect of the Flagellants, who, in an attempt to purge themselves of sin, publicly flogged each other with leather scourges studded with iron spikes until the blood flowed. Penitents rolled in the snow or dust for 33 days because Christ had walked among men for 33 years. Superstition intensified, as did a morbid fancy for everything odious and grotesque. The subject of death itself became an immensely popular preoccupation, expressed in treatises on the art of dying and in paintings on the theme, such as the one in Pisa called *The Triumph of Death (pages 188-189)*.

Between the extremes of mockery and fanaticism, the reaction of most people was to become more introspective about their faith. The art of the post-plague era reflected its brooding spirit.

Sinopia drawings such as this detail of an angel carrying a soul in Traini's *Triumph of Death (opposite page)* could not provide an artist with direct guidelines for his finished work because they were plastered over before the painting began. But they did give him an idea of how his overall scheme would look on the wall, allowing him to check composition and perspective, make changes and, if necessary, show the donor of the mural what he was spending his money on. For the final painting, artists normally worked from sketches on paper, although some masters are believed to have carried the entire plans for their frescoes in their heads.

O ne quickly apparent effect on art, however, was a curiously practical one. Far and wide the plague was held to be God's punishment for assorted sins. Overwhelmed by a sense of guilt and by the need to expiate it, people sought a way out by yielding up wealth often dubiously amassed. Churches and religious confraternities enjoyed a rush of donations and bequests. Much of this went into building and decorating, with consequent full employment for the artist.

Perhaps fittingly, the chief Florentine beneficiary of such largesse was the Compagnia dei Laudesi di San Michele, a benevolent society composed of some of the city's wealthiest merchants. From a wide variety of repentant donors, the Compagnia acquired a windfall of 350,000 florins. It devoted much of this sum to the enhancement of the edifice of Or San Michele, most notably to the construction of a sumptuous marble tabernacle for the interior by Andrea di Cione, called Orcagna, since Giotto's death one of the leading artists of Florence.

Or San Michele's name was a contraction of San Michele in Orto, so called for an ancient church to the Archangel Michael which had stood in a garden—*orto*—on the same site. The church had given way to a loggia where grain was bought and sold, with an enclosed upper story where it was stockpiled for public distribution in the event of war or famine. On one of the loggia pillars was a frescoed Madonna with supposed miraculous powers. No miracle had averted a popular riot at Or San Michele during one famine in which grain officials had employed guards with ax and block to chop off rioters' hands and feet on the spot. Still, the Madonna was widely revered, and when she was badly damaged in a fire, a new Madonna was painted on wood panel by Bernardo Daddi, and placed inside the loggia. Orcagna's tabernacle was commissioned in 1349 as a shrine to house this work.

His labors stretched over 10 years, cost a staggering 86,000 florins, and convinced the sponsors that Or San Michele itself should be remodeled to match. Even before the tabernacle was completed, the grain market was moved elsewhere. The arches of the loggia were subsequently walled up, and the building was converted into a hall church, with two naves of equal height. Well into the next century its walls, both inside and out, provided a backdrop for the talents of Florentine painters and sculptors. Among its later glories, in niches on the exterior, were two monumental marble statues of St. Mark and St. George by Donatello, carved with all the classical majesty beloved by the Renaissance.

Orcagna's tabernacle combines the solidity and austerity of Florentine art with Gothic motifs. It is pinnacled and ornate, as elaborate a paean to the Madonna as any French cathedral in her name. Imposing in size—about 32 feet high and 26 feet wide at its base—it is also dazzling in its ornamentation, combining marble, mosaic, enamel and gilded glass. Every form of the stonecutter's art was brought into play: the incised carving of intaglio, statuettes, reliefs. The front of the tabernacle (*page 185*) forms an altar. Around the base are scenes in relief of the life of the Virgin, beginning with her birth and ending with a rare scene of the "Second Annunciation," in which an angel informs the aged Mary of her impending death. On the back of the tabernacle is a relief in two parts, showing the Virgin's death and Assumption. In the grieving, despairing faces and gestures of the Apostles and spectators, Orcagna movingly captured the spirit of his times.

Among acts of expiation, Orcagna's sculptured masterpiece was surely one of the most spectacular. Yet there was another, quieter way in which survivors of the Black Death sought to express, through the visual images of art, a new spirit of humility and repentance. Giotto had stressed the human qualities of the sacred personages of Christianity; he had shown them in situations recognizable to his viewers. This warm familiarity now vanished. Once again, as in the hieratic paintings of the generations before Giotto, the sacred personages were portrayed as aloof, severe, admonitory rather than compassionate.

Sometimes they were depicted in the act of rendering judgment, sometimes—more subtly—in the mood of contemplating it. In one altarpiece, the Florentine painter Giovanni del Biondo showed a harshly vengeful John the Baptist with his feet planted upon the supine body of the sinful Herod (*page 176*). More intrinsically effective—both as an embodiment of judgment implied, and as a work of art—was an altarpiece executed by Orcagna between 1354 and 1357 for the Strozzi family chapel in the Church of Santa Maria Novella.

As gifted a painter as he was a sculptor, Orcagna boldly set aside convention and devoted the central panel of his altarpiece to a remarkable portrayal of a stern-visaged Christ—no longer the Man of Sorrows, but the Ruler and Judge of all mankind *(pages 186-187)*.

The Strozzi altarpiece holds a distinct hint of another strong trend of the times—the triumph of orthodoxy. The most zealous guardians of Church doctrine were the Dominicans. Santa Maria Novella, where Orcagna painted his work, was in the care of the Dominican order. And so, in Orcagna's altarpiece, Christ is shown handing to St. Thomas Aquinas, the great 13th Century Dominican philosopher and author of the *Summa Theologica,* a book in which is incorporated the wisdom of the ages. Behind the kneeling saint stands the Madonna, with one hand on his shoulder signifying her sponsorship, with the other hand presenting him to her Son.

In another part of Santa Maria Novella, the Spanish Chapel, the Dominicans achieved a more complete triumph of dogma through art. The chapel was munificently endowed by the merchant Buonamico di Lapo Guidalotti, who financed not only its construction but the frescoing of all four walls and ceiling. Andrea Bonaiuti, better known as Andrea da Firenze, was the painter assigned to the work, in 1366. Manifestly he was guided every inch of the way by the Dominican fathers.

On the ceiling and altar wall are variations on a number of traditional religious themes. Covering the other walls are three stupendous frescoes decrying the dangers of heresy and expounding the joys of orthodoxy. One fresco depicts scenes from the life of St. Peter Martyr, the Dominicans' most vigorous heresy-hunter. Another records the apotheosis of St. Thomas Aquinas. The third points the right road to salvation *(pages 190-191)*. The chapel decoration as a whole represents an allegory on this theme. Hundreds of figures and scores of vignettes crowd together in a vast visual encyclopedia. This kind of didactic, propagandizing art is a far cry from the beautifully human way in which Giotto told the religious story. Andrea completed his opus about six decades after Giotto laid down his brush at the Arena Chapel. But the distance from the clarity and concentrated power of the earlier work seems infinite.

Almost six decades more were to pass before Florence saw the rise of a giant equal to Giotto: Tommaso di Ser Giovanni di Mono, better known by his nickname Masaccio, or "Hulking Tom." The conservatism of art in the interim did not extend to technical matters; skills in modeling the figure, in giving expressiveness to the face, in rendering perspective, not only survived but advanced. But it fell to Masaccio—in a brilliant career cut short by his death at 27—to see humanity plain, as Giotto had seen it, and to interpret it with the same elemental grandeur.

With Masaccio, Giotto's art found new soil in which to thrive. It has never since ceased to give sustenance. The medieval world ended and the modern world began; men of many different philosophies and styles of art continued to draw on the essential principles of the Tuscan master. Millions of words have paid him tribute. The simplest and truest, perhaps, were voiced a century ago by John Ruskin. Giotto, he said, "painted what no man could look upon without being the better for it."

Giotto grew up in a time of peace and prosperity, which his art reflected. But after his death things began to go badly for his native region, and with this turn of events art changed too. First, the Florentine bankers in London were forced into bankruptcy when the English, engaged in an expensive war against France, could not pay their debts. Florence's great Bardi and Peruzzi fortunes toppled and the city's economy rocked. At the same time, a long and fruitless military action against Lucca caused further depletions in Florence's treasury as well as its manpower. Tuscany's capacity to import food, often in short supply, was seriously impaired, and when crop failures due to heavy hailstorms followed, the region was weakened immeasurably.

Finally, early in 1348, came the most stunning blow of all: the plague. By August over half the population of Florence—some 50,000 people—and two thirds of the citizens of Siena were dead. The Black Death, so called because dark spots appeared on the victim's skin, caused a dramatic change in the thinking of survivors, who felt that the dreadful scourge was God's punishment for man's earthly sins. Art, following this turn of mind, became dour, harsh and didactic, reverting to the austerity and otherworldliness of a century before. For some fifty years it reflected a sense of mourning, self-reproach and misery, and it was not until the Renaissance that Giotto's humanizing influences were remembered again.

Art in the Shadow of Death

In the guilt-ridden aftermath of the plague of 1348, rich penitents donated huge sums for art to local churches. Sculptor-painter Orcagna was paid 86,000 florins for this magnificent tabernacle of marble and colored inlays, which houses a Madonna and Child by Bernardo Daddi, a follower of Giotto.

Orcagna: *Tabernacle,*
1352-1359

S·MICHAEL·S·KATGRINA·VIRG   ＆·TIRIA·S·THOMAS·DGAQUINO   ANTONIN·CCCLVII·ANDRCAS·CIONIS·DGFLORGTIA·NGPIXIT

STA. MARIA NOVELLA, FLORENCE

ΕΤ·S·PETRVS·PPLS·   S·LAVRENTIVS·S·PAVLVS·PPI

Following the disasters of the plague, religious feeling ran deep and troubled, reverting to a kind of fundamentalism that stressed obedience, redemption of the faithful, and punishment of sins.

Sensitive to this mood, Andrea di Cione, called Orcagna, who painted the altarpiece shown here, depicted Christ as a commanding figure in the act of disseminating Church doctrine and granting ecclesiastical authority. This was a new role for the Savior. In previous panel paintings, He had been portrayed as an infant, or as He suffered on the Cross. Here, He has taken charge of the Church and appears as the omnipotent King. Orcagna's design is also an innovation in that Christ is the central figure, seen seated full-length and surrounded by seraphim.

In the central section, Christ is pictured extending to St. Thomas Aquinas and St. Peter the book and keys, symbols of their roles. At the left, Mary introduces Thomas, the learned theologian and teacher, acting as his sponsor and, symbolically, as an intercessor for mankind. At the right, John the Baptist, an austerely painted near-replica of Christ, stands behind Peter, the militant churchman, as he receives the keys of the earthly Church. At the far left of the composition are St. Catherine, and St. Michael with a dragon at his feet. At the far right are St. Lawrence and St. Paul.

Beneath the main figures, three long rectangular scenes in the *predella,* or base panel of the altarpiece, show episodes from the lives of the saints. The entire work, richly decorated with gold leaf, was given to the Church as a penitential gesture by the wealthy Strozzi family—bankers who may have had some doubts about their own salvation because of the fine line they trod between legal interest and usury.

Orcagna: *Strozzi Altarpiece,* 1354-1357   187

CAMPOSANTO, PISA

Attributed to Francesco Traini: *The Triumph of Death*, probably c. 1350

The horrors of death were nowhere so vividly pictured as in this fresco attributed to Francesco Traini, fittingly painted for Pisa's Camposanto, or town cemetery. Medieval religious thought had long stressed life's shortness and the inexorability of death. But recent memories of lingering sickness and death's capricious selectivity caused a particularly graphic resurgence of this feeling following the epidemics that struck Italy repeatedly between 1340 and 1374.

Unfortunately the fresco *(left)* was severely damaged by fire in World War II. Nevertheless, it still presents a vivid panorama of life and death. In the skies angels and devils struggle for souls *(detail, lower right)*. In the lower right-hand corner of the fresco, elegant young men and women attempt to find a few moments of amusement despite the bat-winged figure of death that hovers near them. At the center, a devil snatches a soul—represented by a child—from the mouth of a man *(detail, center below)*. At the left, a handsomely dressed riding party *(detail, lower left)* comes face to face with three corpses. Only the hermit at the far left, whose scroll cautions against the temptations of pleasure, and the studious and hard-working monks outside the monastery above him, remain serenely untouched by the grim realities about them.

Among the largest and most unusual works commissioned in the wake of the plague is this 30-foot-high fresco, one of a series by Andrea da Firenze that covers the walls of a chapel in Florence. The scene, didactic in the extreme but filled with charming details of contemporary life, depicts the way to salvation—specifically, the way preached by the Dominican monks, who felt that the Church had been entrusted to their care.

At the bottom left, lined up before Florence's great cathedral (Giotto's bell tower is visible at left) are the guardians of the Church, including a bishop with his crossed staff, a red-hatted cardinal, a pope, an emperor, a king and a knight. The sheep sitting in front of the pope are guarded by black and white *domini canes,* "hounds of God"—a punning reference to the Dominicans, who wore black and white robes and were regarded as guardians of the faith.

At the bottom right are St. Peter and St. Thomas Aquinas preaching to the heretics, and St. Dominic, who directs the *domini canes* to attack the wolves who endanger the sheep. Above these saints, surrounding four seated figures that represent earthly pleasures, are innocent young people dancing, playing music and enjoying the fruit of the field. (The dancing girls recall those in the fresco on pages 174 and 175—except that they are more subdued, fitting the mood of the scene.) In the central area of the fresco St. Dominic guides the saved, after their confession to a seated priest, through the gates of Paradise where St. Peter welcomes them. Waiting behind the gates is an assemblage of saints and Biblical heroes.

Christ prevails over the whole scene in Heaven, surrounded by angels but detached from the activities below. This is an accurate reflection of the philosophical attitude toward Christ after the plague; He is no longer pictured as the warmly compassionate Savior of Giotto's Arena Chapel, but as a stern and omnipotent ruler who is to be obeyed and worshiped through His agents on earth, the Church and the Dominican order.

Andrea da Firenze, *The Way of Truth,* 1366 -1368

SPANISH CHAPEL, STA. MARIA NOVELLA, FLORENCE

APPENDIX

Chronology: Artists of Giotto's Era

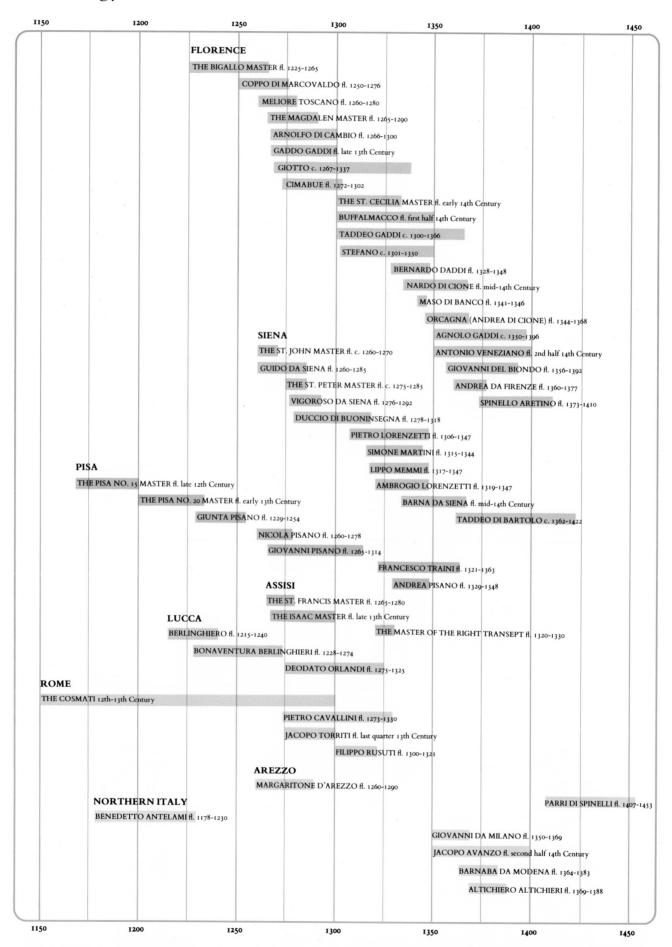

Giotto's predecessors, contemporaries and successors are grouped here in chronological order according to region. The colored bands correspond to the life-spans of the artists or, where this information is unknown, to the approximate periods when they flourished (indicated by the abbreviation "fl.").

Bibliography   *Paperback.

GIOTTO, LIFE AND WORK

Battisti, Eugenio, *Giotto.* Albert Skira, Geneva, 1960.

Carli, Enzo, *Giotto and His Contemporaries.* Crown Publishers, 1958.

Carrà, Carlo, *Giotto.* A. Zwemmer, London, 1925.

Cecchi, Emilio, *Giotto.* Translated by Elizabeth Andrews. McGraw-Hill, 1960.

De Selincourt, Basil, *Giotto.* Charles Scribner's Sons, 1905.

Gioseffi, Decio, *Giotto Architetto.* Edizioni di Comunità, Milan, 1963.

Gnudi, Cesare, *Giotto.* Translated by R. H. Boothroyd. Aldo Martello Editore, Milan, 1960.

Mather, F. J., "Giotto's St. Francis Series in Assisi Historically Considered." *The Art Bulletin,* XXV, 1943, pp. 97 ff.

Meiss, Millard, *Giotto and Assisi.* New York University Press, 1960.

Offner, Richard, "Giotto, non-Giotto." *The Burlington Magazine,* June 1939, pp. 259 ff.; Sept. 1939, pp. 96 ff.

Perkins, F. Mason, *Giotto.* George Bell & Sons, London, 1902.

Rintelen, Friedrich, *Giotto und die Giotto-Apokryphen.* Müller Verlag, Munich, 1912.

Ruskin, John, *Giotto and His Works in Padua.* Charles Scribner's Sons.

Salvini, Roberto:
    All the Paintings of Giotto. Translated by Paul Colacicchi. Hawthorn Books, Inc., 1963.
    Giotto, Bibliografia. Fratelli Palombi, Rome, 1938.

Sirèn, Osvald, *Giotto and Some of His Followers.* Translated by Frederic Schenck. Harvard University Press, 1917.

Tintori, Leonetto, and Eve Borsook, *The Peruzzi Chapel.* Harry N. Abrams, Inc., 1965.

Vigorelli, Giancarlo, *L'Opera Completa di Giotto.* Rizzoli Editore, Milan, 1966.

ART-HISTORICAL BACKGROUND

Antal, Friedrich, *Florentine Painting and Its Social Background.* Routledge and Kegan Paul Ltd., London, 1947.

Borsook, Eve, *The Mural Painters of Tuscany.* Phaidon Press, London, 1960.

Carli, Enzo:
    Duccio di Buoninsegna. Aldo Martello Editore, Milan.
    Italian Primitives, Panel Painting of the 12th and 13th Centuries. Harry N. Abrams, Inc., 1965.
    Sienese Painting. New York Graphic Society, 1956.

Crichton, G. H., *Romanesque Sculpture in Italy.* Routledge and Kegan Paul Ltd., London, 1954.

Crowe, J. A. & G. B. Cavalcaselle, *A New History of Painting in Italy.* E. P. Dutton & Co., 1908.

DeWald, Ernest T., *Italian Painting 1200-1600.* Holt, Rinehart and Winston, 1961.

Fry, Roger Eliot, *Vision and Design.** Meridian Books, 1963.

Garrison, Edward B., *Italian Romanesque Panel Painting.* L. S. Olschki, Florence, 1949.

Gombrich, E. H., *The Story of Art.* Phaidon Press, London, 1957.

Janson, H. W., *History of Art.* Harry N. Abrams, Inc., 1962.

Marcucci, Luisa, and Emma Micheletti, *Medieval Painting.* Translated by N. E. Scott. The Viking Press, 1960.

Meiss, Millard, *Painting in Florence & Siena After the Black Death.** Harper Torchbooks, 1964.

Morey, Charles Rufus, *Mediaeval Art.* W. W. Norton & Co., Inc., 1942.

Nicholson, Alfred, *Cimabue, A Critical Study.* Princeton University Press, 1932.

Offner, Richard, *A Critical and Historical Corpus of Florentine Painting.* J. J. Augustin.

Paccagnini, Giovanni, *Simone Martini.* Aldo Martello Editore, Milan.

Pope-Hennessy, John, *Italian Gothic Sculpture.* Phaidon Press, London, 1955.

Rice, David Talbot, *Art of the Byzantine Era.* Thames and Hudson, London, 1963.

Robb, David M. and J. J. Garrison, *Art in the Western World.* Harper & Row, 1963.

Rowley, George, *Ambrogio Lorenzetti.* Princeton University Press, 1958.

Stubblebine, James, *Guido da Siena.* Princeton University Press, 1964.

Tintori, Leonetto, and Millard Meiss, *The Painting of the Life of St. Francis in Assisi.* New York University Press, 1962.

Toesca, Pietro, *Florentine Painting of the Trecento.* Pantheon, Florence, 1929.

Van Marle, Raimond, *The Development of the Italian Schools of Painting.* Martinus Nijhoff, The Hague, 1923.

Vasari, Giorgio, *The Lives of the Painters, Sculptors and Architects.** Translated by A. B. Hinds. J. M. Dent & Sons Ltd., London, 1963.

Weigelt, Curt, *Sienese Painting of the Trecento.* Pantheon, Florence, 1930.

White, John, *Art and Architecture in Italy 1250-1400.* Penguin Books, Inc., 1966.

CULTURAL AND HISTORICAL BACKGROUND

Bergin, Thomas G., *Dante.* Orion Press, 1965.

Bishop, Morris, *Petrarch and His World.* Indiana University Press, 1963.

Boccaccio, Giovanni, *The Decameron.* Translated by Richard Aldington. Garden

(Bibliography continued on page 194)

A Key to Duccio's "Maestà" (See Pages 76-79)

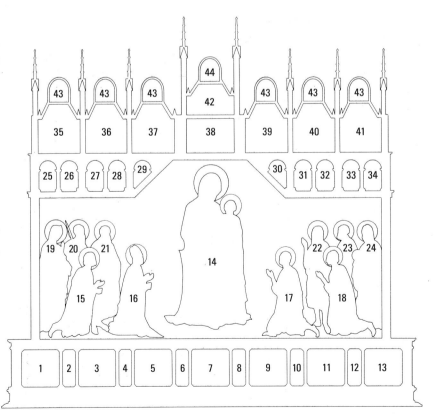

1   *The Annunciation*
2   *The Prophet Isaiah*
3   *The Nativity*
4   *The Prophet Ezekiel*
5   *The Adoration of the Magi*
6   *The Prophet Solomon*
7   *The Presentation of Christ in the Temple*
8   *The Prophet Malachi*
9   *The Massacre of the Innocents*
10 *The Prophet Jeremiah*
11 *The Flight into Egypt*
12 *The Prophet Hoseah*
13 *Christ Disputing with the Doctors*
14 *The Madonna and Child*
15 *St. Ansanus*
16 *St. Savinus*
17 *St. Crescientius*
18 *St. Victor*
19 *St. Catherine*
20 *St. Paul*
21 *St. John the Evangelist*
22 *St. John the Baptist*
23 *St. Peter*
24 *St. Agnes*
25 *St. Thaddeus*

26 *St. Simon*
27 *St. Philip*
28 *St. James the Great*
29 *St. Andrew*
30 *St. Matthew*
31 *St. James the Less*
32 *St. Bartholomew*
33 *St. Thomas*
34 *St. Matthias*
35 *The Annunciation of the Virgin's Death*
36 *The Virgin Mary's Farewell to St. John*
37 *The Virgin Mary's Farewell to the Apostles*
38 *The Dormition of the Virgin Mary*
39 *The Funeral Procession of the Virgin Mary*
40 *The Entombment of the Virgin Mary*
41 *The Resurrection of the Virgin Mary*
42 *The Coronation of the Virgin Mary*
43 *Angels*
44 *The Blessing Christ*

Bibliography (continued)

City Publishing Co. Inc., 1930.

Brucker, Gene A., *Florentine Politics and Society 1343-1378*. Princeton University Press, 1962.

Cambridge Medieval History. The Macmillan Co., 1932.

Cantor, Norman F., *Medieval History.* The Macmillan Co., 1963.

Cennini, Cennino D'Andrea, *The Craftsman's Handbook.*★ Translated by Daniel V. Thompson Jr. Dover Publications Inc., 1933.

Cheyney, Edward P., *The Dawn of a New Era 1250-1453.*★ Harper & Brothers, 1936.

Constable, W. G., *The Painter's Workshop.*★ Oxford University Press, 1954.

Coulton, George Gordon, *The Black Death.* R. M. McBride & Co., 1932.

Douglas, Langton, *A History of Siena.* E. P. Dutton & Co., 1903.

Englebert, Omer, *St. Francis of Assisi.* Translated by Marie Cooper. Franciscan Herald Press, 1965.

Ferguson, George Wells, *Signs and Symbols in Christian Art.*★ Oxford University Press, 1954.

Ferguson, Wallace K., *Europe in Transition, 1300-1520.* Houghton Mifflin, 1962.

Ghiberti, Lorenzo, *I Commentari.* R. Ricciardi, Naples, 1947.

Gontard, Friedrich, *The Chair of Peter, A History of the Papacy.* Holt, Rinehart and Winston, 1964.

Heer, Friedrich, *The Medieval World.*★ Translated by Janet Sondheimer. World Publishing Co., 1962.

Huizinga, Johan, *The Waning of the Middle Ages.*★ Translated by F. Hopman. E.

Arnold and Co., London, 1937.

Jacobus de Varagine, *The Golden Legend.* Translated by Granger Ryan and Helmut Ripperger. Longmans, Green & Co., London, 1941.

James, Montague Rhodes (translator), *The Apocryphal New Testament.* Oxford University Press, 1963.

O'Sullivan, Jeremiah, and John F. Burns, *Medieval Europe.* Appleton-Century-Crofts, 1943.

Poston, M. M. & E. E. Rech (editors), *The Cambridge Economic History of Europe.* Cambridge University Press, London, 1963.

Schevill, Ferdinand:
Medieval and Renaissance Florence.★ Harper Torchbooks, 1963.
Siena: The History of a Medieval Commune.★ Charles Scribner's Sons, 1909.

Steegman, Mary G. (translator), *Tales from Sacchetti.* J. M. Dent & Co., London, 1908.

Thompson, Daniel V., *The Materials and Techniques of Medieval Painting.*★ Dover Publications Inc., 1956.

Thompson, James Westfall, *Economic and Social History of the Middle Ages 300-1300.* Frederick Ungar, 1959.

Thompson, James Westfall and Edgar N. Johnson, *An Introduction to Medieval Europe, 300-1500.* W. W. Norton & Co., Inc., 1965.

Villani, Giovanni, *Istorie Fiorentine.* Societa Tipografica de' Classici Italiani, Milan, 1802.

Acknowledgments

The editors of this book are particularly indebted to Jeremiah O'Sullivan, Professor of Medieval History, Fordham University, who read and commented on the complete text. They also wish to thank the following: Don Giulio Bassotini, Sta. Croce, Florence; Luisa Becherucci, Director, Galleria degli Uffizi, Florence; Mario Bernocchi, Prato; Luciano Berti, Soprintendenza alle Gallerie, Florence; Ezio Cantagalli, Opera della Metropolitana, Siena; Enzo Carli, Superintendent, Soprintendenza alle Gallerie, Siena; Muzio Cesari, Vicchio; Renzo Chiarelli, Gabinetto dei Disegni e Stampe, Galleria degli Uffizi, Florence; John Clark, Scala, Florence; Dorothy M. Cogswell, Mt. Holyoke College, South Hadley, Massachusetts; Count Alessandro Contini-Bonacossi, Florence; Eric C. Hulmer, Harmony, Pennsylvania;

Antonietta Morandini, Director, Biblioteca Riccardiana, Florence; Millard Meiss, Institute for Advanced Study, Princeton, New Jersey; Bruno Molajoli, Director of Fine Arts and Antiquities for Italy, Ministero di Pubblica Istruzione, Rome; Rev. Giuseppe Palumbo, S. Francesco, Assisi; Enrico Pistolesi, Opera della Primaziale, Pisa; Giovanni Previtali, Florence; Ugo Procacci, Superintendent, Soprintendenza ai Monumenti, Florence; Alessandro Prosdocimi, Director, Museo Civico, Padua; Mario Ristori, Archivio di Stato, Florence; Marcello Salerni, Municipio, Siena; Silio Sensi, Soprintendenza alle Gallerie, Florence; Matila Simon, New York; Leonetto Tintori, Gabinetto di Restauro, Galleria degli Uffizi, Florence.

Picture Credits

The sources for the illustrations in this book appear below. Credits for pictures from left to right are separated by commas, top to bottom by dashes.

SLIPCASE: SCALA.

END PAPERS:
Front: left Scala, right Alinari (6). *Back:* Alinari.

CHAPTER 1: 6—Alinari. 9—Anderson. 12—courtesy the Vatican Library. 13—Fogg Art Museum, Harvard University, bequest of Hervey E. Wetzel. 14—Biblioteca Medicea Laurenziana, Florence. 15—Walter Daran. 17, 18, 19—Scala. 20—Robert Crandall courtesy George R. Hann Collection, Sewickley Heights, Pa. 21—National Gallery of Art, Samuel H. Kress Collection, Washington, D.C. 22—Scala.—Fratelli Fabbri, Milan. 23—Marzari. 24, 25—Scala. 26, 27—David Lees.

CHAPTER 2: 28—Scala. 32—Alinari photo with line overlay copied from page 141 in *The Paintings of the Life of Saint Francis of Assisi*, Leonetto Tintori and Millard Meiss, New York University Press, 1962. 36—Novosti Press Agency. 41—Bibliothèque Nationale, Paris. 42 through 53—Dmitri Kessel.

CHAPTER 3: 54—Scala. 56, 57—maps by Rafael Palacios. 58—courtesy American Heritage. 63—Foto Grassi, Siena. 67—Scala. 68—Alinari. 69 through 75—Scala. 76, 77—(diagram of panels on page 193) panel 43 left John G. Johnson Collection, Philadelphia; photo by A. J. Wyatt. Panel 43 right S.H.A. Van Heek, s'Heerenberg, Netherlands; photo by Hein de Bouter. Panel 1—The National Gal-

lery, London. Panels 2, 3, 4—The National Gallery, Washington, D.C. Panels 5-13 and 35-40 and main panel—courtesy Museo dell'Opera del Duomo, Siena; photos by Scala, photocomposition by Robert Crandall Associates. 78, 79—Scala.

CHAPTER 4: 80—Aldo Durazzi. 83—Alinari. 85, 86—Alinari. 87—Anderson. 91—Scala. 92 through 99—Alinari.

CHAPTER 5: 100—Scala. 103—Biblioteca Hertziana, Rome—The Metropolitan Museum of Art, Hewitt Fund 1917. 104—Biblioteca Ambrosiana, Milan—Istituto Centrale del Restauro, Rome. 106—Giraudon. 108, 109, 110—Alinari. 111—Scala (2). 113—Scala. 114, 115—Dmitri Kessel. 116—drawing by George V. Kelvin. 117 through 129—Scala.

CHAPTER 6: 130—Scala. 134—Alinari—Gabinetto fotografico del Museo Civico di Padova. 136—Alinari. 138—Tosi, Florence courtesy the Biblioteca Riccardiana, Florence. 139—British Museum. 140—Giraudon. 143—Aldo Durazzi. 144—Scala (2). 145—David Lees. 146, 147—Scala. 148, 149—Marzari, Scala. 150, 151—Scala.

CHAPTER 7: 152—Scala. 157, 158—Alinari courtesy Museo dell'Opera del Duomo, Siena. 159—Scala. 160—Alinari. 162, 163—Bibliothèque Nationale, Paris. 165 through 171—Scala. 172, 173—David Lees. 174, 175—Scala.

CHAPTER 8: 176—Scala. 180, 181—Erich Lessing from Magnum. 185, 186, 187—Scala. 188, 189—Erich Lessing from Magnum. 190, 191—Scala. 192, 193—drawing by George V. Kelvin.

Index

Numerals in italics indicate a picture of the subject mentioned. Unless otherwise identified, all listed art works are by Giotto. Dimensions are given in inches except where indicated; height precedes width.

Index (continued)

The text for this book was set in photocomposed Bembo. First cut in Europe in 1930, Bembo is named for the Italian humanist Pietro Bembo (1470-1547), an arbiter of literary taste. While it has some resemblance to letters designed in 1470 by Nicholas Jenson, it is largely based on characters cut by Francesco Griffo around 1490.

✕✕✕

PRINTED IN U.S.A.